What is Quality in Higher Education?

SRHE and Open University Press Imprint
General Editor: Heather Eggins

What is Quality in Higher Education?

Edited by
Diana Green

Society for Research into Higher Education
& Open University Press

Published by the SRHE and
Open University Press
Celtic Court
22 Ballmoor
Buckingham
MK18 1XW

and

1900 Frost Road, Suite 101
Bristol, PA 19007, USA

First Published 1994

A catalogue record of this book is available from the British Library

ISBN 0 335 15740 8 (pb)   0 335 15741 6 (hb)

Library of Congress Cataloging-in-Publication Data

What is quality in higher education? / edited by Diana M. Green.
    p.   cm.
    Includes bibliographical references and index.
    ISBN 0-335-15741-6   ISBN 0-335-15740-8 (pbk.)
    1. Education, Higher—Great Britain—Evaluation. I. Green, Diana
M., 1943- .
    LA637.W43 1994
    379.1'54—dc20   93-10117
                                                                   CIP

Typeset by Graphicraft Typesetters Limited, Hong Kong
Printed in Great Britain by St Edmundsbury Press,
Bury St Edmunds, Suffolk

Contents

List of Contributors

Jim Finch, formerly Director of Quality, IBM, now quality consultant

Malcolm Frazer, Chief Executive of the Council for National Academic Awards

Diana Green, Pro-Vice-Chancellor, University of Central England in Birmingham

Terry Melia CBE, formerly Senior Chief Inspector, Her Majesty's Inspectorate, now Chief Inspector, FEFC

Baroness Pauline Perry, formerly Vice-Chancellor, South Bank University

Ian Raisbeck, Quality Director, Royal Mail

William H. Stubbs, formerly Chief Executive, PCFC, now Chief Executive, FEFC

Carole Webb, Deputy Director, Division of Quality Audit, Higher Education Quality Council

Preface

It is a truism to say that whereas efficiency was the key word of the 1980s, quality is the touchstone of the 1990s. Concern about quality is not new in the educational context, although much of the debate outside of the sector has focused on standards. Indeed, part of the difficulty which educationists experience in their attempt to demonstrate the quality of the services they are offering rests on the tendency to use quality and standards interchangeably.

In the UK, the absence of any agreed definition has become problematic in the wake of the changes set in train by the 1988 Education Reform Act. Pressure for more accountability in the use of public funds, together with changes to the structure and funding of higher education, designed to increase competition for students and resources, provided the initial rationale for giving quality a higher profile than in the past. The Government's commitment to a higher participation rate together with the decision overtly to tie quality assessment to funding decisions sharpened the concern. However, a fundamental dilemma remains: if there is no consensus about what quality is in higher education, how can it be assessed?

This book was stimulated by, and reflects some of the debate which ensued in the period following the publication of the 1991 Further and Higher Education Bill and its subsequent enactment. Contributions were written, however, before the passing of the 1992 Further and Higher Education Act. It also draws on the preliminary findings of a major national research project, funded by a partnership of government, business and higher education, designed to develop and test methods for systematically assessing quality.

The focus here is on the quality of teaching and learning. Although the quality of research is an important element in assessing the quality of higher education it is not considered here. This is partly because there is a well-tried and tested methodology for its assessment.

Since the publication of the 1991 Further and Higher Education Bill, public attention has focused on the planned expansion of higher education. While this is generally welcomed, concern has been expressed about shifting from the traditional elitist system of higher education to a 'mass' system, analogous to the North American model, together with a stable or falling unit of public resource. How will we know if quality and standards have declined?

The first chapter sets the theme of quality in the broader context. While not answering the question posed, it seeks to examine some of the differing views about how quality might be defined and assessed, drawing on the theory and practice of quality management.

One such perspective, that of one of the Higher Education Funding Councils, is discussed in more detail in Chapter 2. William Stubbs considers the practical advice offered by the Committee of Enquiry set up by the Polytechnics and Colleges Funding Council (PCFC) to look at teaching quality in the context of the changes to higher education, including its relationship to the schools and further education.

The next three chapters present differing approaches to the problem of defining and measuring quality drawn from the British higher education system. In Chapter 4, Terry Melia describes one of the more contentious methods: direct observation of quality in the classroom by an external agency, in this case Her Majesty's Inspectorate. While the Inspectorate will have no role in quality assessment in the new and unified higher education system, it is likely that some element of observation will be retained. As Pauline Perry points out, the introduction of teaching appraisal into the universities has led to considerable refinements in the methods of evaluating the competence of individual teachers. It is axiomatic that assessment should be a major ingredient of appraisal. Whether the two evaluation processes will ultimately converge is a moot point.

In Chapter 5, Carole Webb discusses the introduction and operation of a relatively new technique, quality audit. Like financial audit, on which it is loosely modelled, this technique focuses on the examination of an institution's documented procedures and practices. Initially limited to the traditional universities, the scope of the old Academic Audit Unit (now under the aegis of the Higher Education Quality Council) has been extended to all degree-awarding institutions. One major concern of the universities is the confusion between quality audit and assessment. While the division of responsibility is clear, the potential for overlap and duplication is significant.

An important assumption of the book is that there might be lessons which higher education institutions could learn from organizations with a more business-oriented culture. The chapter by Jim Finch tackles head-on the importance of measurement in any organization committed to continuous quality improvement. Measurement is essential to establish improvement priorities and to measure unequivocally progress made. Ian Raisbeck provides a fascinating case study of a public service organization, Royal Mail, adopting commercial management techniques initially in response to customer dissatisfaction. He describes the organizational and cultural transformation that follows from seeing the customer (internal or external) as at the heart of the progress of continuous quality improvement.

In higher education there is considerable doubt about the applicability of the concepts, values and language of commercial organizations to those providing public services. Nor is it clear whether the customer is the student, the employer or the Government, which funds universities on behalf of the taxpayer. The papers from those within British higher education provide a fascinating glimpse of the extent to which the traditional assumptions, procedures and values are perceived to be shifting.

None of the chapters provides a definitive answer to the question: What is quality? Nor, as Malcolm Frazer points out, can we find any consensus about how quality should be defined and assessed when we look overseas. Moreover, debate about quality is further hampered by the lack of agreement about the meaning of terms relating to quality and standards as well as those relating to those techniques that are designed to assist quality improvement.

Nevertheless, the debate continues. Indeed, the question has become even more pressing and pertinent as the full impact of the latest set of reforms works through the newly unified and more competitive higher education system.

Diana Green

Part 1

What is Quality in Higher Education?

1

What is Quality in Higher Education?
Concepts, Policy and Practice

Diana Green[1]

Qualities too elevated often render a man unfit for society: we don't take ingots with us to market; we take silver or small change. (Nicolas-Sébastien Chamfort, *Maximes et Pensées*, 1796)

'What the hell is quality?' Many of those currently working in higher education and grappling with the increasing pressures to demonstrate that the 'product' they offer is at least as good as that offered by their competitors, must empathize with Christopher Ball's frustrated question.[2] This chapter explores why quality has moved up the British political agenda and considers why some of the current arrangements have been wanting for funds. It also looks at the argument about quality assessment, focusing on the wide variety of *definitions* currently in use, which make agreement on methods of assessment so problematic.

Why the current concern about quality?

Concern about quality and standards is not new. However, until the mid-1980s, any debate was mainly internal to the higher education system. As Moodie points out,[3] the response of academics when the issue became a matter of public concern was bewilderment and a sense of injustice. Underlying this was a surprising confidence in the assumption, reinforced by the earlier Robbins Report,[4] that academic standards were safe in the hands of the universities, and indignation that the integrity of the academic profession should be impugned by the demand for greater public accountability.

Since the mid-1980s, public interest in and concern about quality and standards has been intensified by the increasing attention given by successive British governments to reforming higher education (Table 1.1). The reasons

Table 1.1 Milestones in quality assurance in British higher education

Date	Event	Purpose/Effect
1964	CNAA established	To guarantee quality and standards in the new polytechnic sector
1984–6	Publication of the Reynolds Reports and new academic standards	Introduction of formal quality assurance systems in the universities
1985	Lindop Report on academic validation in the public sector	Responsibility for quality assurance progressively transferred from the CNAA to individual institutions under licence
1987	DES White Paper: *Higher Education: Meeting the Challenge*	Proposal to expand HE. Polytechnics and Colleges to be freed from Local Authority control
1988	Education Reform Act	Polytechnics and Colleges incorporated. Two new funding councils established – UFC for the universities; PCFC for the Polytechnics and Colleges. Quality and price to determine resources allocation
1990	CVCP Academic Audit Unit established	To audit the quality assurance processes of the universities
1991	DES: *Higher Education: A New Framework*	Pledge to expand to be undertaken by abolishing the binary line. Polytechnics to be designated as universities. Audit and assessment of quality were essential
1992	Further and Higher Education Act	Binary line abolished. PCFC and UFC replaced by separate Funding Councils for England, Scotland and Wales. Quality assessment is a statutory responsibility of the HEFCs. HMI's role in HE abandoned. CNAA abolished
1992	HE Quality Council established	Owned by the universities, it takes over the Audit responsibilities of the AAU, and the Access and Quality Enhancement roles of the CNAA

for this growing concern become apparent when we look closely at the policy parameters, the key ones of which are:

1. Rapid expansion of student numbers against a backcloth of public expenditure worries.
2. The general quest for better public services.
3. Increasing competition within the educational 'market' for resources and students.
4. The tension between efficiency and quality.

While the number of people entering higher education grew in the 1970s, this growth was at a relatively moderate rate, constrained, in part, by the very low participation rate in education post-16. During the 1980s, the numbers increased almost wholly as a result of the expanding provision of the polytechnics and colleges. The 1987 White Paper[5] spelled out the Government's view of the main challenge facing Britain in the 1990s. In analysing Britain's poor economic performance relative to her major competitors it was apparent that the participation rate in further and higher education was considerably lower. Logic dictated that in order to exploit the potentially competitive advantages of new scientific and technological developments and the new international division of labour, a larger workforce was needed, with more advanced knowledge and skills. Putting this simply, a better educated workforce would lead to greater economic success. This view has been confirmed by a recent Industrial Research and Development Advisory Committee (IRDAC) report on skills shortages in Europe.[6]

However, a potential brake on these expansion plans was the very high cost of education in Britain. Demographic trends, which suggested a significant increase in the proportion of the elderly and dependent in the overall population, together with a determination to keep public expenditure under control, meant that the only way the circle could be squared was by getting 'more for less'. The resources available for higher education had to grow at a slower rate than the participation rate. Higher education institutions must therefore demonstrate the same efficiency gains as other public sector institutions.

This change in approach was dictated not only by financial considerations but also by the ideological and philosophical approach of Conservative governments. This is underlined by the use of language, concepts and practices hitherto unknown in the educational context. The search for economy, efficiency and value for money assumes a degree of management totally foreign to the traditional democratic and collegiate culture of the universities. In this respect, the Government's approach to higher education can be seen as part of its general determination to improve public services. Institutions should not only be more efficient, they should also be more responsive to the needs of their customers, and accountable to the taxpayer.

The British Government's approach to educational reform springs from this ideological stance. While education will never strictly speaking be a 'free' market, nevertheless an injection of market forces should engender the kind of behaviour, essentially competition for students and resources, which is conducive to greater efficiency. It is interesting to compare the response of institutions in the two sectors in the wake of the 1988 reforms. Each Funding Council adopted a different funding strategy, in part reflecting the differing traditions and styles of governance in the old polytechnic and traditional university sectors. Thus the Polytechnics and Colleges Funding Council (PCFC) incorporated a more overt form of competition, by incorporating in its methodology an element of competitive bidding. It also fulfilled its remit of taking quality as well as price into consideration in its resource allocation decisions by encouraging competition for quality 'flags', symbols of outstanding quality (adjudicated by Her Majesty's Inspectorate) with an added financial 'bonus'. Similarly, when the Government decided to promote expansion and lever greater efficiency by the simple expedient of shifting a proportion of the funds from the Funding Councils to the tuition fees that flow automatically with each full-time or sandwich student, it was the PCFC institutions that responded to the incentive by increasing recruitment. The response of the universities to 'fees only students' was initially cautious and sceptical: more energy was spent defending the 'unit of resource' in the interest of maintaining quality and standards.

Nevertheless, the results overall were impressive: by 1991, one in five 18-year-olds were entering higher education, compared with one in seven a decade before. However, it was not enough. The 1991 White Paper[7] therefore signalled an ambitious target: a participation rate of one in three by the year 2000. This was to be achieved by removing what was seen to be the biggest barrier to expansion: the binary line. Granting the polytechnics the right to use the university title and confer their own degrees would remove their 'second division' status creating a 'level playing field' which would facilitate genuine competition.

There are two related fears. First, there is concern about the impact on standards of 'overcrowding', as a result of pressure on staff, student ratios, equipment, library resources and space. Second, there are concerns about the impact on standards of a 'dilution' of the quality of the intake. This is articulated in the idea that 'more means worse'. It has been exacerbated by an increase in the proportion of those entering higher education who do not fit into the standard A level entrance classification, as institutions have given greater weight to broadening access criteria.

Interest in quality is also explained by, and is a product of, higher education's response to the demand for greater efficiency. Thus, there is a genuine fear that in the competition for students and resources, quality will be traded for greater efficiency. Efficiency gains have been achieved largely by changes in the approach to teaching and learning. Examples include the development of modularization and credit accumulation schemes, the abandoning of the individual tutorial and small group teaching, the development of student-centred learning approaches, where the staffing input shifts from that of teacher to facilitator and the development of more 'imaginative' forms of assessment, including peer assessment. Some of these developments can be seen as positive insofar as they produce real gains for the students. Thus modularization and credit accumulation offer flexibility over time and space and enhance access opportunities, meeting the needs of a more heterogeneous student population. These developments may also facilitate a small shift in the balance of educational purposes, from initial to continuing education and professional updating. However, many employers are concerned about these changes. While welcoming the possible benefits of recruiting from a larger pool of graduates, they nevertheless have two related concerns. First, increased entry into higher education may lead to a lower standard of knowledge and no real increase in the transferable skills that they value so highly. The fear here is that larger numbers will mean a dilution of the content of the educational process. At the same time, they are concerned about what the development of a 'mass higher education' system will mean. Looking at the product of higher education in the United States, they see a bewildering variety of institutions, each with a different 'mission', producing graduates with qualifications of variable quality. They are genuinely concerned about their ability to make informed choices when recruiting graduates if the British system develops along the same lines.

Central to the debate about quality in the educational context is the issue of whether concepts derived from the profit-centred private sector can be readily transferred to public service organization. It is argued that commercial organizations are funded differently, have different objectives and face a different external environment. One example of this philosophical divide is the reaction of most academic institutions to the notion that students might be seen as 'customers'. The debate about who are the 'customers' or 'stakeholders' in higher education is very much informed by the argument about concepts of quality which is considered later. However, despite these philosophical and practical difficulties in transplanting business techniques and practices to higher education,[8] there is evidence that some transference has occurred. Examples include a growing interest in marketing techniques, which is visible *inter alia* in the development of corporate styles and logos, the revamping of prospectuses, the production of corporate videos and the proliferation of higher education fairs where universities, polytechnics and colleges quite literally set their stalls up and market their wares to potential recruits at home and overseas. Indeed, the notion of 'market share', in this case the share of total applicants, has become an important performance indicator. In competitive markets, quality is seen as a vital tool for those organizations wishing to maintain current market share or secure a competitive advantage. While subjective factors like 'reputation' and 'image' are important, businesses are increasingly seeking more objective ways of demonstrating their superior quality relative to their competitors. This phenomenon explains the growing popularity of quality management systems such as BS 5750 or total quality management (TQM). Interest in such systems is beginning to percolate from the manufacturing sector to public service organizations in fields like health and education. At present, most of the interest in these techniques seems to be in further education. In higher education, the greatest area of actual and potential interest is in continuing vocational education and professional updating.[9]

Implicit in the push for competition between institutions is the risk that in the search for a greater share of student numbers and resources, quality will be sacrificed. To head off any criticism of declining academic standards, the 1991 White Paper and subsequent Act of Parliament require the funding councils to establish quality assessment units to inform their funding decisions.

Quality of what?

Leaving aside for the moment what definition of quality the funding councils should be using, we need to consider what aspect or dimension of higher education should be assessed. In so far as it has a general mission or purpose of underpinning (national) economic and social development by providing the skilled manpower required, this mission is fulfilled by two related activities:

1. Producing graduates to meet the human resource needs of organizations in the business, industrial and service sectors (including public services).
2. Pushing forward the frontiers of knowledge via research.

The European Memorandum on Higher Education[10] suggests that as far as the latter is concerned, institutions should be engaged in different types of research with outputs ranging from technology transfer and marketable products to the pursuit of knowledge for its own sake. It is for this reason that the linkage between the quality of teaching and research in higher education institutions must be stressed. Historically, British universities have been funded on the assumption that the two functions are inextricably linked. An element of their block grant has underpinned research and provided them with the critical mass (in respect of human and physical resources) that supported competitive bidding for additional research funds from the research councils and other public or private sources. Since 1989, the funding of research has been subject to a series of changes designed to concentrate public funds in a select number of institutions, essentially those that produce the best 'return' on the public investment in the shape of the highest quality of research output. This change has four key features:

1. The progressive separation of teaching and research.
2. The progressive transfer of research funds from the universities' block grant, distributed by the funding council, to the research councils. This increases both the transparency of funding and the element available on a competitive basis.
3. The progressive reduction of the scope of research funding by clarifying the boundaries between 'pure', 'strategic' and 'applied' research. While the former can be funded legitimately out of the public purse, the assumption is that 'applied' or 'near-market research' should be funded by the market.

4. The assessment and ranking of research outputs by subject area and institution, and the use of these rankings to underpin a more selective approach to research funding.

At the time of writing, the third exercise has just been completed. It differed from previous ones to the extent that it was extended to the 'new' universities, i.e. the polytechnics and the colleges of higher education, which previously had not received funding for research. The political logic is obvious: abolition of the binary line means that new and old universities will be funded by the same funding council. They should therefore be assessed against the same rules governed by the same criteria. As expected, the newcomers have gained only a modest share of the research cake, given their relative inexperience in this type of exercise, their different 'missions' and the fact that a larger number of institutions were competing for a smaller envelope of resources.

Within higher education, the research assessment exercise provoked considerable controversy, notably about the effect on institutions of the ranking exercise and the assessment methodology. The clear intention was to separate, on a subject area basis, those institutions that are centres of research excellence from those that have a teaching mission. The financial implications of poor ratings both directly, through the funding council grant, and indirectly, in respect of the capacity to bid successfully for research council or other funding, is a source of increasing concern. At the same time, criticism of the assessment exercise seems to be focused on the link between ranking and funding. There has been relatively little criticism of the assessment criteria *per se*. Moreover, the peer review system on which assessment is based seems to have been broadly accepted as the most reliable and well established method of providing independent judgement about the quality of research output.[11]

Quality of teaching

Assessing the quality of the other main educational mission, the production of graduates, is a much more difficult and complex task. Are we mainly concerned with the quality of inputs (human and physical resources), outputs (graduates) or the process of teaching and learning itself?

There is no single answer. Indeed, the answer will depend on who is making the judgement and for what purpose. Table 1.2 shows some of the methods and the agencies currently responsible for quality assurance and quality control as far as teaching and learning are concerned. While the precise focus of interest may vary from agency to agency, it is clear that there is also considerable overlap. To take one example: in the case of an undergraduate degree in accountancy, the university or college offering the course and the relevant professional body will each have an interest in the quality of staff teaching the course. However, the focus of their interest may be different. As far as the university or college is concerned, the key question will

Table 1.2 Assessing the quality of teaching and learning: methods in use prior to the 1992 Act

Action	Responsible agency	Method and focus
Validation or course approval	CNAA or the institution offering the course/programme	Appraisal of inputs and design of course/programme as against specified aims and appropriate standards
Course review	CNAA or the institution offering the course/programme	Evaluation of the process and output against initial specification
Accreditation	CNAA or a professional body	Evaluating the appropriateness of an institution to offer programmes leading to specified award. (Inputs, outputs and process considered)
Audit	Academic Audit Unit of the CVCP	Examining and commenting on the Universities' quality assurance systems (inputs and process)
Inspection	Her Majesty's Inspectorate	Similar to accreditation but with an emphasis on student experience in the classroom
Performance indicators	Funding Councils, accrediting bodies, individual institutions	Quantitative or qualitative methods of assessing quality (inputs, outputs or process) and standards
Moderation	External examiners	Monitoring output to ensure comparability with national academic standards

be whether the staff are qualified to deliver the programme of study to the appropriate (national) academic standard. The professional body will be concerned with the professional competence of staff if the programme of study is to confer on the graduate professional recognition. As recent research has shown, each stakeholder is likely to have a different perspective on the contents of the undergraduate programme, especially the balance between subject-specific knowledge and transferable skills. Table 1.2 also illustrates the fact that higher education already spends a considerable proportion of its resources on quality assurance. Indeed, part of the explanation for the current dissatisfaction with existing procedures is that they are both ineffective and costly.

While it is generally accepted that quality assurance is a legitimate cost, many institutions are concerned about the heavy investment required to support a plethora of overlapping control systems.

At the heart of most approaches to quality assurance is evaluation by experts, generally known as peer review. This is an umbrella term used indiscriminately to describe all the methods that involve human judgement; whether or not the judgements are informed by less subjective data and irrespective of whether those making the judgements are peers.[12] Peer review is increasingly being challenged in the context of discussion about teaching quality on the grounds that the subjective nature of the judgements renders their reliability questionable. This concern increased after 1988 when quality judgements began to have a direct bearing on funding decisions. The concern was most explicit in the PCFC sector, specifically when the decision was taken to recognize and reward those institutions that could substantiate claims of outstanding quality. Arguably, the fact that the Council for National Academic Awards (CNAA) refused to adjudicate claims and that HMI was eager to fulfil this function, helped hasten the demise of both. At a more fundamental level, the exercise highlighted both the difficulty of defining outstanding quality (let alone distinguishing it from 'poor', 'satisfactory', 'good' or high quality) and finding an objective test.

There is clearly a correlation between the breakdown of the traditional peer-review-based quality assurance system and the increasingly market-oriented culture of higher education. In a competitive rather than a collegiate system, it is difficult to distinguish academic evaluation from self-interest. Similarly the trust and confidence that underpinned the process of forming collective views about the quality of individual programmes of study has been eroded by the growing suspicion that course evaluation will provide a backdoor route to teaching appraisal.

The retreat from the subjectivism of peer review has resulted in a growing interest in performance indicators. These exist in many forms and categories,[13] an account of which is beyond the scope of this paper. A useful definition is supplied by Cuenin:[14] performance indicators are described as empirical quantitative or qualitative data that are relative rather than absolute and imply a point of reference that enables an assessment of achievement against a defined objective. In practice, quantitative indicators are found more commonly than qualitative ones and very few indicators that genuinely help evaluate teaching quality have been developed.[15] Most are concerned with efficiency (e.g. staff–student ratios, unit costs, space utilization); cost-effectiveness (e.g. completion rates, graduate employment rates) or some form of proxy for quality (e.g. student or client satisfaction).[16]

The main advantages of performance indicators (PIs) is their usefulness for making comparisons between institutions, departments or courses over time. Their disadvantages are numerous and well known. These include: validity – the tendency to measure what is measurable rather than the parameter of performance that is of interest, the need to explain and qualify and the tendency to affect behaviour in unintended ways (e.g. to secure high scores by lowering standards in order to reduce drop-out rates). Despite their weaknesses, PIs do produce a (superficially) simple way of indicating the health of the educational system. At the same time, it seems likely they will be used, via the publication of 'league tables' of comparative performance, to inform potential customers of relative quality and to reinforce the competitive ethos of higher education desired by government.

From quality assurance to quality assessment

The 1991 White Paper stated that quality assessment units would be expected to provide information about 'the actual and relative quality of institutions and the courses they provide'.[17] Quality assessment is seen as separate from academic audit from the perspectives of purpose, methodology and institutional responsibility. While audit focuses on the robustness of quality assurance and quality management systems, and is therefore legitimately the responsibility of the institutions themselves, it is a statutory obligation of the new funding councils to consider, and therefore assess, the quality of the provision of those institutions funded from the public purse. The Government's motive in requiring such assessment is clear: it is essential if the fears about a decline in quality and standards as a result of combining expansion with a falling public unit of resources are to be challenged.

Quality assessment is a controversial proposal. There are several related reasons for this, including:

1. Who will carry out the assessments?
2. What criteria will be used?
3. What will be the relationship between audit and assessment?
4. Will the cost of external accountability reach unacceptable levels, thereby reducing the institution's ability to invest in quality improvement?

Behind the arguments is the more fundamental concern: what is quality in the higher education context? Without some agreed definition of its 'essential nature', how can the task of quality assessment be carried out? However, a single substantive definition of quality is not possible. As one recent study reminds us, the one figure who almost found such a definition went crazy when he found it, leaving us with the famous quotation 'But when you try to say what quality is, apart from the things that have it, it all goes poof! There's nothing to talk about.'[18]

Concepts of quality in higher education

Quality, like 'freedom' or 'justice', is an elusive concept. We all have an instinctive understanding of what it means but it is difficult to articulate. Quality is also a value-laden term: it is subjectively associated with that which is good and worthwhile.[19] For this reason it is claimed by many to validate or justify an activity, and sometimes with scant attention to what the word might mean. This makes it difficult to disentangle how the word is being used in a particular circumstance. Nevertheless, it is both desirable and feasible to identify a number of different approaches. The following section, which draws on preliminary research on quality assessment,[20] pulls together some of the differing concepts in use in the current arguments about how quality in the higher education concept might be assessed.

The traditional concept of quality

The traditional concept of quality is associated with the notion of providing a product or service that is distinctive and special, and which confers status on the owner or user. Extremely high standards of production, delivery and presentation are set, which can only be achieved at great expense or with the use of scarce resources, thus putting them out of reach of the majority of the population. The notion of exclusivity is implied.[21]

The exemplar often used is that of the Rolls Royce. In higher education, it might equate with most people's perception of Oxford and Cambridge Universities, both in terms of the distinctive and special student experience that they provide, and in terms of the graduate and research output. However, this concept of quality is not of much value when it comes to assessing quality in higher education as a whole. If all institutions were judged by the same criteria as those used to judge Oxford and Cambridge, most would be continually condemned as poor quality. Even if it were possible to make every institution like Oxford and Cambridge, would it be desirable?

Conformance to specification or standards

Second, there is the notion of quality as conformance to a specification or standard. This approach has its origins in the notions of quality control in the manufacturing industry.

It is, perhaps, worthwhile being totally clear about what the term 'standard' means in this context. It is a basis for measurement, or a 'yardstick' – a neutral term to describe a required characteristic of a product or service.

The specification for a product or service comprises a number of standards. The quality of the product or service is measured in terms of its conformance to the specification. Quality control in this context relates to testing the product or service to see whether it meets the standards set and rejecting those that do not conform.

This type of approach to quality is currently fashionable in the public services. It underpins the recent introduction of a number of 'customer charters', seen by the Government as a means of increasing the accountability and responsiveness of public service providers. Examples include the Parents' Charter in relation to education and the Patients' Charter in relation to the health service. Each contains a series of service standards, which, if met, produce a quality service for the 'customer'.

This approach to quality has an advantage over the earlier definition in its application to higher education. It gives all institutions an opportunity to aspire to quality, as different standards can be set for different types of institution. Under this definition, it is perfectly possible to have a poor quality Rolls Royce and a high quality Mini.

The disadvantage with this model is that it tells us nothing about the criteria used to set the standards and, unless the standards are in line with our understanding of what is significant, we may not agree that something is a quality product or service, even if it conforms to the standards that have been set for it (the British Rail standard for a train being on time – arriving within 15 minutes of the scheduled arrival time – is an example here).

It is also an essentially static model,[22] as it implies that once a specification has been defined it does not need to be reconsidered. As the pace of technological change in society increases, however, it seems likely that services and products will need to be revised to reflect new circumstances.

Finally, it implies that the quality of a service can be defined in terms of standards that are easily measurable and quantifiable, and this may not be the case in higher education.

The use of the term 'standard' causes other difficulties in relation to higher education, as it is often used in a different sense to that defined above: it is used to mean excellence or a high standard.[23] When the word is used in this context it is sometimes difficult to be clear what is being talked about. A concern that standards are dropping may be taken to mean either that the level of achievement required to pass a course has been lowered, or that students are achieving a lower level of performance even though the standard (in the more neutral 'yardstick' sense of the term) remains the same.

In some circumstances, academic standards in terms of student achievement appear to be equated with quality in higher education, as in the following statement by Kenneth Clarke when he was Secretary of State for Education and Science:[24]

> The statistics speak for themselves, with the proportion of graduates in PCFC sector institutions gaining first and upper seconds having risen alongside the surge in student numbers. There are plenty of examples from HMI to show how increasing numbers need not adversely affect quality – quite the reverse.

Sometimes the term 'academic standards' is used just in relation to the output of higher education in terms of student achievement, as in the example described above. However, it may also be used in a much broader sense in relation to the whole range of activities concerning teaching and learning and research in higher education including admissions procedures, the content of courses, methods of delivery, physical resources and so on.

In analysing quality in relation to higher education it is therefore important to be clear how the term 'standard' is being defined and applied.

Quality as fitness for purpose

The definition of quality adopted by most analysts and policy makers in higher education is that of fitness for purpose.[25] Exponents of this approach argue that quality has no meaning except in relation to the purpose of the product or service. Quality is judged in terms of the extent to which a product or service meets its stated purpose(s).

This definition, therefore, provides a model for determining what the specification for a quality product or service should be. It is also developmental, as it recognizes that purposes may change over time, thus requiring constant re-evaluation of the appropriateness of the specification. It may be used to analyse quality in higher education at a number of levels. For example, if the purpose of higher education is to provide an appropriately educated workforce, is the system as a whole providing the right number of graduates? Is a particular course providing the right balance of knowledge, skills and understanding? Is an institution achieving the purposes it set for itself in its mission statement?

The problem with this definition of quality in higher education is that it is difficult to be clear what the purposes of higher education should be. In recent years, few attempts amongst policy makers to define the purposes of higher education have gone beyond that provided by the Robbins Committee,[4] which stated that the objectives of higher education were 'instruction in skills', 'promotion of the general powers of the mind', 'advancement of learning' and 'transmission of a common culture and common standards of citizenship'. The 1987 White Paper[26] took this definition and added to it an emphasis concerning meeting the needs of the economy. However, different stakeholders in higher education may have different views about this issue. Who should define the purposes of higher education? Should it be the government, the students, the employers of students, the managers of institutions or the academic professionals? It is theoretically possible that all these groups would concur on the purposes of higher education, but more likely that there would be at least some differences of opinion.

Finally, higher education may have multiple purposes, some of which are conflicting. How would these conflicts be resolved in judging the quality of an institution? Who would determine the priorities?[27]

Quality as effectiveness in achieving institutional goals

One version of the 'fitness for purpose' model concentrates on evaluating quality in higher education at the institutional level. A high quality institution is one that clearly states its mission (or purpose) and is efficient and effective in meeting the goals that it has set itself. This approach can be seen in a number of instances. For example, the Committee of Vice-Chancellors and Principals (CVCP) Academic Audit Unit made it clear that it started from the premise that there is no 'gold standard' in higher education.[28] The individual universities determine their own definitions of quality and standards and the Academic Audit Unit, through its audit process, sought to evaluate whether the quality assurance system that the university has established was successfully achieving its aims and objectives.

This view of quality is also implied in the 1991 White Paper *Higher Education: A New Framework* in terms of the Government's desire to ensure that new funding arrangements for teaching should be 'related to and safeguard the best of the distinctive missions of individual institutions' and in the pressure to develop performance indicators.

This model has significant implications for higher education as it broadens the spectrum of issues deemed relevant to the debate about quality to include performance in areas such as efficiency in use of resources or effective management.

Quality as meeting customers' stated or implied needs

During the last 20 years, the definition of quality most often used in industry has evolved and is no longer given solely in terms of conformance to a specification but in terms of meeting customers' needs. High priority is placed on identifying customers' needs as a crucial factor in the design of a product or service. In Deming's terms 'the difficulty in defining quality is to translate future needs of the user into measurable characteristics, so that a product can be designed and turned out to give satisfaction at a price that the user will pay'.[29]

Using this definition of quality, it is clear that fitness for purpose should be related to customers' needs. Yet there are a number of complications in defining quality as meeting customers' needs, particularly in the public service sector.

Who is the customer in higher education? Is it the service user (the students) or is it those who pay for the service (the government, the employers)? Is the student the consumer, the product or both?

Taking the view that it is the service user, or student, who is the customer raises a number of difficulties, particularly in the evaluation of the service. While it may be relatively easy to identify the physical needs of students in higher education in terms of access to adequate library provision and adequate student accommodation, the heart of the education service is the relationship between the lecturer and student in the teaching and learning process. Unlike the manufacturing industry, the producers and customers (lecturers and students) are both part of the production process making the process individual and personal, depending on the characteristics of both the producer and the consumer. The result of these characteristics is that standards of quality are difficult to state and maintain. In some cases services are not only physically but mentally intangible, because they are difficult to grasp and understand.[30]

Some critics of this approach to defining quality in relation to higher education ask whether students are in a position to know what their needs are.

They may be able to identify their short term needs, but do they have enough knowledge and experience to know what they need in the long term? Are they in a position to judge whether their needs are being met?[31]

The usual response to this issue is that satisfying students' needs is not the same as satisfying their wants.[32] It also points to the need to make an analytical distinction between different concepts of quality and the best methods for assuring or assessing quality. Defining quality as meeting customers' needs does not necessarily imply that the customer is always best placed to determine what quality is or whether it is present. This definition, therefore, also leaves open the question about who should define quality in higher education and how it should be assessed.

The pragmatic definition of quality in higher education

Given the difficulties in defining quality in higher education, some have opted out of trying to find an underlying theory or definition.[33] Vroeijenstijn (1991) says 'it is a waste of time to try to define quality'.[34] The basis of this argument is that quality is a relative concept, that different interest groups or 'stakeholders' in higher education have different priorities and their focus of attention may be different.[35] For example, the focus of attention for students and lecturers might be on the process of education, while the focus of employers might be on the outputs of higher education. It is not possible, therefore, to talk about quality as a unitary concept, quality must be defined in terms of qualities, with recognition that an institution may be of high quality in relation to one factor but low quality in relation to another.

The best that can be achieved is to define as clearly as possible the criteria that each stakeholder uses when judging quality, and for these competing views to be taken into account when assessments of quality are undertaken.

Conclusion

In the last resort quality is a philosophical concept. Definitions of quality vary and, to some extent, reflect different perspectives of the individual and society. In a democratic society there must be room for people to hold different views: there is no single definition of quality that is right to the exclusion of all others. Indeed, we may catch ourselves switching from one perspective to another without being conscious of any conflict.

Even if we opt for one definition of quality, say 'fitness for purpose', the conclusions that we reach when interpreting this notion for higher education would depend on our values and our priorities. The outcomes might be very different, depending on who defines the purpose.

Reaching the conclusion that we might all have different understandings of quality in higher education and that none of us is necessarily wrong or right does not mean, however, that we are absolved of the responsibility for maintaining and enhancing quality. In practical terms, decisions have to be taken: courses have to be approved or turned down, funding has to be allocated, new lecturers have to be appointed in competition with others.

It is an argument for greater transparency. In other words, all those called on to make judgements about the quality of the teaching and learning process, or its output, should seek to clarify the criteria on which such judgements are made, irrespective of the purpose of making those judgements. The articulation of the criteria used in a transparent and public way is unlikely to produce agreement about their relative importance. It is thus unlikely that any single method of assessment will emerge to satisfy the purposes of all the interested parties making the judgements.

This points to the need for the development of a framework that will clearly articulate the relationship between the criteria used and the various quality assurance and quality management techniques currently available, whether within or without higher education, in Britain or overseas. This should provide a stronger, more reliable, and more credible basis for quality assessment than that which currently exists.

Notes and references

1. The section on concepts of quality draws heavily on the preliminary research undertaken by Alison Burrows and Lee Harvey as part of a national project on Assessing Quality in Higher Education (QHE), which was launched in 1991. The project is supported by a partnership of 27 organizations from government, business and the public service sector.
2. Ball, C. (1985) What the hell is quality? In *Fitness for Purpose – Essays in Higher Education*. Guildford, SRHE and NFER/Nelson.
3. Moodie, G.C. (ed.) (1986) Fit for what? In *Standards and Criteria in Higher Education*. Guildford, SRHE and NFER/Nelson.
4. Robbins, L. (1963) *Report of the Committee on Higher Education*, Cm 2154. London, HMSO.
5. DES (1987) *Higher Education: Meeting the Challenge*, White Paper Cm 114. London, HMSO.
6. European Commission (1991) *Memorandum on Higher Education in the European Community*, 5 November. Brussels, Commission of the European Communities.
7. DES (1991) *Higher Education: A New Framework*, White Paper Cm 1541. London, HMSO.
8. Pollitt, C. (1990) Doing business in the temple? Managers and quality assurance in the public services. *Public Administration*, 68 (Winter), 435–52.
9. De Wit, P. (1992) *Quality Assurance in University Continuing Vocational Education*. London, HMSO.
10. European Commission (1991), see note 6.
11. See, for example, Boden (1990) *Peer Review: A Report to the Advisory Board for the Research Councils from the Working Group on Peer Review*. London, ABRC.
12. CNAA, CHEPS, HIS (1992) *Towards a Methodology for Comparative Quality Assessment in European Higher Education*. CNAA, London.

13. See, for example, PCFC (1990) *Performance Indicators: Report of a Committee of Enquiry*, chaired by A. Morris. London, PCFC; HMI (1990) *Performance Indicators in Higher Education*, a Report by HMI, Ref. 14/91/NS, January–June. London, DES; Cave, M., Hanney, S., Kogan, M. and Trevett, G. (1991) *The Use of Performance Indicators in Higher Education: A Critical Analysis of Developing Practice*, 2nd edn. London, Jessica Kingsley; Yorke, M. (1991) *Performance Indicators: Observations on their Use in the Assurance of Course Quality*, CNAA Project Report 30. London, CNAA.

14. Cuenin, S. (1986) International study of the development of performance indicators in higher education. Paper given to OECD, IMHE Project. In Cave, M., Hanney, S., Kogan, M. and Trevett, G. (1991) *The Use of Performance Indicators in Higher Education: A Critical Analysis of Developing Practice*, 2nd edn. London, Jessica Kingsley.

15. Weert, E. de (1990) A macro analysis of quality assessment in higher education. *Higher Education*, 19, 57–72.

16. Mazelan P., Brannigan, C., Green, D. (1991) Using measurers of student satisfaction: the implications of a user-led strategy of quality assurance in higher education. *Broadcast* (Journal of the Scottish Further Education Unit), 18 (Winter), 4–5.

17. DES (1991), see note 7.

18. Pirsig, R.M. (1976) *Zen and the Art of Motorcycle Maintenance: An Inquiry into Values*. London, Corgi.

19. Dochy, F.J.R.C., Segers, M.S.R. and Wijnen, W.H.F.W. (1990) Preliminaries to the implementation of a quality assurance system based on management information and performance indicators. In Dochy, F.J.R.C., Segers, M.S.R. and Wijnen, W.H.F.W. (eds) *Management Information and Performance Indicators in Higher Education: An International Issue*. Maastricht, Van Corcum.

20. Research undertaken as part of a national project on Assessing Quality in Higher Education (QHE), launched in 1991. The project is supported by a partnership of 27 organizations from government, business and the public service sector.

21. Pfeffer, N. and Coote, A. (1991) *Is Quality Good for You? A Critical Review of Quality Assurance in the Welfare Services*. London, Institute of Public Policy Research.

22. Walsh, K. (1991) Quality and public services. *Public Administration*, 69(4), 503–14.

23. Moodie, G.C. (1986), see note 3.

24. DES (1991) Clarke tells polytechnics to plan for changes next year. *Department of Education and Science News*, 17 September.

25. See Ball, C.J.E. (1985), note 2; CVCP of the Universities of the United Kingdom (1986) *Academic Standards in Universities*, with introduction by P.A. Reynolds. London, CVCP; HMI (1989a) In pursuit of quality – an HMI view. In *Quality in Higher Education: An HMI Invitation Conference*, 16–18 June, Heythrop Park; Crawford, F.W. (1991) *Total Quality Management*, CVCP Occasional Paper. London, CVCP.

26. DES (1987), see note 5.

27. Billig, B. (1986) Judging institutions. In Moodie, G.C. (ed.) *Standards and Criteria in Higher Education*. Guildford, SRHE and NFER/Nelson; Taylor, W. (1981) Quality control? Analysis and comment. *Educational Administration*, 9(2), 1–20.

28. CVCP of the Universities of the United Kingdom, Academic Audit Unit (1990), see note 25.

29. Deming, W.E. (1982) *Out of the Crisis – Quality, Productivity and Competitive Position*. Cambridge, Cambridge University Press.

30. Walsh, K. (1991), see note 22.

31. Roberts, D. and Higgins, T. (1992) *Higher Education: The Student Experience. The*

Findings of a Research Programme into Student Decision Making and Consumer Satisfaction.
Leeds, HEIST.
32. Marchese, T. (1991) *TQM Reaches the Academy* (unpublished paper). American
Association for Higher Education.
33. Dochy, F.J.R.C., Segers, M.S.R. and Wijnen, W.H.F.W. (1990), see note 19.
34. Vroeijenstijn, T.I. (1991) External Quality Assessment: Servant of Two Masters?
Paper presented to the Conference on Quality Assurance in Higher Education,
15–17 July, Hong Kong.
35. Harvey, L. and Green, D. (1993) *Defining quality. Assessment and Evaluation in Higher
Education*, 18(1), 9–34.

2

Quality in Higher Education: A Funding Council Perspective

William H. Stubbs

Defining quality in higher education

Why quality?

Ten years ago, the title of a book like this probably would not have been 'what is quality in higher education' but something rather narrower and more parochial, such as 'what do we mean by academic standards?' This is the very question the then Secretary of State, Sir Keith Joseph, put in 1983 to the Chairman of the University Grants Commission (UGC). It could even have been the more arcane question: 'what is validation?'

Obviously, the 1988 Education Reform Act is one cause of a number of changes in the context of higher education. Alternatively, however, the Act can be seen as much as a symptom of wider changes than as a cause of them. It enshrines in legislation changes concerned with:

- increasing market orientation;
- value for money;
- price and quality as factors in resource allocation;
- concern for market share;
- consumer satisfaction.

All of these changes have been felt particularly acutely in the manufacturing and service industries, commerce and in the public services. They constitute also international rather than strictly national developments.

In industry, the debate now goes beyond the inspection of products when they are made to looking at the processes of the production itself and the organizational climate in which it takes place. In academia too, interest has widened beyond standards to quality.

Thus the earlier concern with the examination of standards, which has connotations of levels of attainment by students on entry and at graduation, is being overlaid by a broader interest in what happens in between these two events.

Other reasons for the emphasis on quality in higher education can also be advanced:

1. The greater scale of the higher education enterprise in 1990 compared with 1980. Ten years ago in institutions in England and Wales the total home student population was 553,000 (excluding the Open University). In 1989, the total was estimated to be 752,000, a 50 per cent increase. One per cent of the nation's gross domestic product (GDP) is now spent in support of higher education.
2. The increased range of educational attainment of students entering higher education for the first time. The A level route still predominates but increasingly more entrants have other qualifications.
3. The popularity of modular courses with students and a consequent decline in the proportion of graduates with single honours degrees. The diversity of subject content makes assessments by employers more difficult.
4. The increasing importance of part-time courses and hence in the participation of older students. This is accompanied by changes in the experiences and expectations of students.
5. The effect of the recognition that the quality of research in universities is variable.

All these factors reinforce the impression that the quality of higher education, unlike mercy, can be considered as strained and dropping unevenly on the ground of academe.

PCFC and quality

In response to the guidance given by the Secretary of State to the PCFC, the Council incorporated 'quality' explicitly within the criteria that underpinned its funding methodology in conjunction with demand and price. It has also stated that it was committed to 'promoting the provision of quality higher education'. In 1989, the Council established a Committee of Enquiry to advise it (and the institutions that it funds) on the quality of teaching and how quality improvement might be promoted.

The committee spent some time debating how to define 'quality'. It was eventually concluded that there was not one single definition but, rather, that 'teaching, like other activities, will be judged good by whether or not it contributes to the achievement of purpose; and that higher education has a variety of purposes, though all of them related to the life chances of the student'.[1] Thus, instead of searching for one ingredient which ensured the presence of 'quality', the committee sought to identify the 'qualities' of teaching that might be generally accepted as making that teaching of a quality that was distinctive. Accordingly, the committee identified a number of under-lying principles and a number of necessary conditions.

Three underlying principles were identified:

- 'Teaching' must be interpreted broadly.
- Teaching must be responsive to students' needs.
- The conditions necessary for good teaching must be taken seriously, their satisfaction given priority at every level of institutional activity.

The committee then identified five necessary conditions, namely that:

1. There should exist clarity of aims and objectives related specifically to teaching, and confidence that they are worthwhile and appropriate to students' needs.
2. There should be a policy regarding curriculum organization and delivery, including a readiness to consider different methods of promoting learning.
3. There should be a policy for the professional development of teaching staff, including appointment, induction, appraisal and development.
4. There should be means by which the views of students and employers can be used in judgement of the curriculum, its delivery and outcomes.
5. There should be an identifiable framework within which an institution can evaluate its own success in meeting its objectives and adjust its practice accordingly.

If the PCFC were to be satisfied that quality of teaching is being taken seriously in an institution, each of these conditions should be met.

Widening the definition – and the definers – of quality in higher education

The trends that the Committee identified and that led it to define quality as it did are part of the wider contextual changes to higher education.

First, the definition of quality and the circle of those involved in framing the definition is widening as the range of students and purposes widens. Inevitably, the views of funding agencies, such as the Training and Enter-prise Executive of the Department of Employment (TEED), through the Enterprise Initiative, are becoming more influential and the views of students are being sought out and considered. In addition, employers, both as employers of graduates and as proxies for wider society, are becoming more vocal. Through the work of agencies like the Council for Industry and Higher Education, their views are becoming expressed in ways that academics can appreciate and to which they can respond.

Those who consider that this absence of a specific definition of quality on the part of the committee is a weakness may have missed this groundswell. The committee's approach focuses the challenge to institutions in a particular direction: that is, not at defining quality but at doing something about it. The focus is on the actions that teachers, students, employers and institutional managements will have to take in order to ensure that the quality of teaching is indeed high.

Second, the range of quality management tools is also widening. Thus, BS 5750, which was developed initially for the manufacturing sector, sets out a management system for quality assurance which many companies have adopted. Some further and higher educational institutions are now seeking to apply it to themselves. This system specifies that to be successful a company must offer products or services that:

- meet a well defined need;
- satisfy customers' expectations;
- comply with applicable standards and specifications;
- comply with statutory and other requirements of society;
- are available at competitive prices;
- yield a profit.

The company should organize itself so that all factors under its control are orientated to the reduction, elimination and prevention of quality deficiencies.

Total quality management (TQM) is a similar approach which tries to ensure quality by involving everyone in the enterprise in active concern for it. Consequently, total quality is assumed to mean that the processes by which the product is produced, in the industrial context, become the assurance of a quality product. Thus, we see adverts for Japanese cars identifying aspects of Eastern philosophy and relating these to the organizing principles of the factory and its quality assurance (rather than control) processes. It is not so much the medium becoming the message, more that the medium of production becomes part of the product.

Just as BS 5750 is concerned with the relevant and appropriate quality management systems, rather than the product itself and its post-production inspection, so quality in higher education is about how an institution organizes itself to deliver quality teaching rather than the *ex-post-facto* measurement of the standard achieved by the student. Quality is thus wider than standards: quality becomes the experience of the student as much as his/her degree classification. Academic standards are therefore no longer synonymous with teaching quality.

The committee's five necessary conditions for teaching quality focus directly on the actions needed to reflect and take forward the changing context of higher education. They take forward ideas about accountability, about specification of delivery in exchange for public funds, about involving employers, about listening to and responding to student views and about the framework within which all these things can be put into practice.

What is vital is both what the institution does and how it does it – 'doing the right things right', as Deming has said.[2] A number of questions then arise:

1. What is the right thing?
2. What is doing it right?
3. How do we know either or both are being achieved?

If an institution is to answer these questions, it must have the appropriate mechanisms and the involvement of all its staff, students and wider circle of employers, and local community.

The Teaching Quality Committee used slightly different words to give the same basic message. It argued that to be good, teaching must contribute to the achievement of a variety of purposes. It follows from this that:

1. *The right thing* can best be approached by specifying those aims and objectives that could be confidently felt to be appropriate to students' needs (the committee's first necessary condition for good teaching). Peter Drucker's book *Managing the Non-Profit Organization*[3] gives as the first premise for success a precise definition of an organization's purpose.
2. *Doing that right* requires a policy for curriculum organization and delivery (the committee's second necessary condition).
3. *Both* student and employer views are essential to knowing whether what is being done is 'right' (third and fourth necessary conditions).
4. All these could only be wrapped up in a framework for self-evaluation, by the institution, that goes beyond meeting the conditions as much to a concern for the everyday life of the institution that makes the student experience there qualitatively different (fifth necessary condition and strategy to the Council).

Other contextual changes

The Government has made plain its determination to increase the participation rate in higher education without any decline in standards:

> The Government is now committed both to further expansion and to the maintenance and, if possible, the enhancement of standards. Institutions therefore need to be ready to teach an increased number of students and also those who come to them with different backgrounds and expectations. No institution can be content with old practices even if these have been successful in the past. They must, above all, show themselves to be flexible and to be responsive to their students.

The PCFC Committee on access teaching quality wrote:

> We have already emphasised the need to attract students from more varied backgrounds and the need for flexibility and responsiveness in ensuring that the curriculum is accessible to them. Students must be

encouraged to think critically about teaching methods and how they learn and to join in devising ways of learning which suit them. They must be encouraged to recognise that the aim of the institution is to meet their educational needs, and that this is not possible without their active participation. Indeed it is to be seen as part of their higher education that they learn to be critical and imaginative about their own learning, both what they are learning and how they may best learn it.

This leads on to the relationship between higher education, schools and further education. One of PCFC's principal objectives up to 1993 was to promote mutually beneficial links between institutions in the sector and secondary schools, colleges of further education and other institutions of higher education in this country and, increasingly, overseas.

In support of that objective, the Council sent a copy of Teaching Quality Report to every sixth form and further education college in the country, some 4000 institutions. A number of themes stood out in the responses:

• That higher education institutions should be aware of and sensitive to the changes in the content of the school curriculum.
• That increasingly students will enter higher education with the ability to learn independently because of changes in the way in which pupils are coming to learn in schools.
• That students feel they spend a lot of time going over things already covered in the school curriculum.
• That the quality of pastoral care and attention in higher education sometimes lets them down.

Let me conclude with a recent quotation[4] from Philip Reynolds, a former Vice-Chancellor of University of Lancaster, where he draws attention to the different observers of the quality of higher education:

To the committed scholar the quality of higher education is likely to be determined by its ability to produce a steady flow of people with high intelligence and commitment to learning who will continue the process of transmission and advancement of knowledge. To a Secretary of State a high quality system may be one that produces trained scientists, engineers, architects, doctors and so on in numbers judged to be required by society. To an industrialist in the British tradition a high quality educational institution may be one that turns out graduates with wideranging, flexible minds, readily able to acquire skills and adapt to new methods and needs. The measurements required, and thus the standards to be applied will be different for each of these notions of quality.

It is considerations such as these that lead inevitably to interest in the quality of the whole system; the quality of an institution and the quality of the individual course.

References

1. PCFC (1990) *Teaching Quality.* (Report of a Committee of Enquiry).
2. Deming, W.E. (1982) *Out of the Crisis – Quality, Productivity and Competitive Position.* Cambridge, Cambridge University Press.
3. Drucker, P. *Managing the Non-Profit Organisation.*
4. Loder, C.P.J. (1990) *Quality Assurance and Accountability in Higher Education.* Kogan Page.

Part 2

Models from Within
British Higher Education

3

Defining and Measuring the Quality of Teaching

Baroness Pauline Perry

Upon the education of the people of this country, the fate of this country depends
(Disraeli, 1874)

If the 1980s was the decade when the public services were driven towards
greater efficiency, cost-consciousness and value for money, then the 1990s
seem fair set to be the decade of quality. In the natural course of events, when
the measures for increased efficiency have been applied for a period of time,
the question properly arises as to the target for the quality of service which
is being provided. I have argued elsewhere[1] that quality is not an absolute,
even in the education service, nor do we do well to encourage the public to
believe that, in this respect, education is different from the other goods and
services they buy and receive. The woman who buys a Mini may well commend it for the quality of its workmanship, and her pleasure in its man-
oeuvrability in city traffic. She does not, however, expect it to perform as a
Rolls Royce would perform, and her expectations of quality in her Mini are
very different from the expectations she would have towards a Rolls Royce.
In other words, quality is related to price, and our satisfaction with the
quality of goods or services depends entirely on the legitimate expectations
we had towards them at the time of purchase. To put it another way, it is
fitness for the purpose which we judge, and which defines the quality we
expect and approve.

Quality and diversity

This is as true for higher education as it is for commercial goods and services. It would be wholly inappropriate to expect the models of Oxford and
Cambridge to determine our expectations towards all higher education in the
United Kingdom. Indeed, it can be argued that a vague and ill-defined belief
that there is something absolute in, for example, the quality of the British first
degree, has been a hindrance and not a help to our development as a modern

advanced society in the latter part of the twentieth century. Accepting that the target for quality standards will vary from one institution to another, throws into sharper relief the importance of the mission statement. Here again, the mystique of absolute quality, and the mystique of the old universities, has for too long obscured the differing missions of the many higher education institutions in the United Kingdom. It will greatly enhance the provision of the future if we accept that every institution will develop its own unique mission, which in turn will determine its ethos, the nature of its offerings and the nature of its particular market share of students and sponsors. It is perhaps not popular to say, but nevertheless I believe it to be true, that differing aims and the differing definitions of quality resulting from them, are quite properly reflected in the differing prices that we as higher education institutions charge. With or without a Government policy change, it seems inevitable that the next decade will see a break in the concept of equal fees for all undergraduate courses across all institutions. As in the United States and many other countries, prestigious institutions will find ways of charging higher fees, in order to raise revenue, and undoubtedly they will find many students and their parents only too willing to pay. We must hope that the universities who choose this course will remain sufficiently committed to the concept of academic excellence that they continue to find routes, via scholarship and sponsorship, to enable highly talented students of modest means to enrich their student population.

The arguments for diversity of aims and mission are incontrovertible, if we consider the diversity of needs in society and of individual students, which the higher education system is increasingly gearing itself to meet. In the 1940s and 1950s, it was possible to conceive of the higher education system as catering to an economically and academically elite group within society, who in turn would become the social and academic elite of adult life.

The tiny proportion of every age group of 18-year-olds who moved on to higher education was destined for the teaching profession, the Civil Service and the upper echelons of a few large industrial and commercial concerns. Britain lagged behind the rest of the world in expecting the economy to thrive on a labour force that was, in the main, educated only to the age of 15. Not until the 1970s was the school leaving age raised to 16, and even then only a tiny minority chose to stay on to A level in order to move, at 18, into the more respectable professions of banking and the like. Not until the mid-1970s were the teachers in primary and secondary modern schools (and this included the teachers of the less able pupils in comprehensive schools) expected to have two A levels before entry into their teacher training courses, which at the same time were transformed into undergraduate courses leading to the Bachelor of Education (BEd) degree.

Education and international competition

Fortunately, although later than any other leading Western nation, the British Government has now encouraged wider access into higher education, and has set a target of 30 per cent of the age group entering higher education within the early part of the twenty-first century. It is worth remembering that France, Sweden, Japan, the USA and many other Western countries reached this target 15 years ago. Consequently, we shall be more than a generation behind them in providing a workforce within which a sizable proportion has been educated beyond the age of 18.

It is not only the major Western nations that have progressed beyond even our current plans. Indeed, John Naisbitt, author of the Megatrends Series, has noted that 'In the world economy, education is the Pacific Rim's competitive edge.'[2] Already one-third of Korean young people go on to university, and in both Korea and Taiwan the national commitment to education exceeds or matches that of every developed country except the United States and Japan. Korea has the highest number of PhDs per capita in the world, and one of its major enterprises, the Daewoo Group, employs about 1000 people with PhDs. We cannot afford to plan simply for an expansion of undergraduate education. Major enterprises abroad now take it for granted that their senior personnel, in general management as well as in technical areas, will have qualifications above a first degree. In many ways, we are in danger of making the mistake of thinking 20 or 30 years behind our competitors, if we do not now plan to expand our postgraduate work in line with the expansion of undergraduate higher education. The important thing, however, is that providing higher education for this much wider range of individual needs and future placement in the workforce, requires a much wider diversity of offerings in higher education, both in terms of the nature of the institutions, and the nature of the courses which they offer. Definitions of purpose and mission derived from the 1950s simply will not fit the appropriate mission for a higher education system catering to 20 or 30 per cent of the population. We are indeed no longer producing only the solo players, but rather the dedicated and talented members of the economy's orchestra. Some universities must still provide the solo performers, for every society needs them. However, society needs a far larger number of the good orchestral members, capable of performing with professional skill while remaining positive members of a creative team. The majority of higher education institutions should be geared towards seeking out such talent, and applying their efforts to producing skilled and professionally trained team players.

Quality of teaching

It is because of this that the new emphasis on teaching quality should be applauded. As numbers of those participating in the higher education system increase, and as that increase is inevitably unmatched by an equal increase in unit funding, the quality and versatility of teaching will become ever more important. Stories have reverberated for decades about poor teaching by academics who were distinguished in research but failures when it came to communication of their knowledge to students. Such stories were treated with gentle tolerance when the students were part of a gifted elite and could compensate by their own efforts for the very mediocre teaching they sometimes received. As the gates widen, the nature of the student body becomes more varied, albeit more in relation to the educational backgrounds they have experienced than to the innate talent they possess. Consequently, teaching will have to be highly skilled and appropriate to the diverse needs of the student population. Nor will the employers of the future continue to tolerate the graduate who has a 'well rounded and trained mind' but whose knowledge and skills are unrelated to the needs of the economy. Training such generalist graduates absorbs large quantities of time and resources within the company. Many employers are beginning to ask why the higher education system has not used its own resources more effectively to develop appropriate knowledge and skill in its graduates.

The nature of teaching will need to become not only more varied and versatile, but will also have to be of a very high quality. Strangely, although the nature of high quality teaching is not an absolute, and will necessarily vary with the subject, mode, level and size of group being taught, yet in the meta-language of judgement, the criterion that high quality teaching should meet the needs of individual students is an absolute. The interaction between a doctoral student and tutor in English, for example, is of a very different nature from the interaction between the tutor and a class of 15 first year undergraduates in a science laboratory. Yet each could be judged of high or low quality, in so far as the teaching does or does not meet the needs of the individual students concerned.

The ultimate guarantee of quality in the interaction process must be in the attitudes, knowledge and skills of the individual teachers themselves. Teachers who feel enthusiasm for their job, and who are well qualified and expert in what they teach, are the only essential ingredients in teaching quality. It is for those who lead the academic teachers to provide the ethos and a real sense of autonomy for each individual, in order to release their creative talent in teaching. Nevertheless, it is also the responsibility of management to know what the quality of student experience is in the department, faculty or institution for which they are responsible. Reaching a judgement about the skill of each individual teacher must therefore be part of management responsibility, and senior academic leaders must develop ways of collecting evidence about teaching quality.

Observation of the teaching process is an essential part of the process in formulating judgements of quality. However, observation in the classroom is a highly skilled task, and there are few senior managers in higher education who would feel competent to undertake it themselves. Increasingly, higher education institutions are putting in post people who can take responsibility for the quality of teaching throughout the institution. Many of these include a friendly and supportive style of classroom observation in their work. Her Majesty's inspectors were, in the past, the most important external body to sit in classrooms, and make professional judgements about the quality of the teaching that they saw. The Inspectorate has no role in the new unified higher education system. But within the institution it may well be that more informal and supportive observation has to be combined with external performance indicators. It is possible to formulate a judgement of an individual's teaching competence with sufficient accuracy to include it in the teacher appraisal process that is now being instituted in universities. There is no question that such an assessment must be a major ingredient of the appraisal. In default of skilled observation, the external performance indicators will certainly include the standard of students' work, the drop-out rates, performance of the group of students taught by the member of staff concerned as measured against the average for the course and the department, the level of degree performance and the success of students in achieving employment. I see no reason why measures of student satisfaction should not regularly be taken in quite formal written questionnaires. These too should be used to measure the adequacy of an individual teacher's performance.

Evidence from far too many sources indicates that the higher education system still contains, and tolerates, too large a minority of teachers who are not delivering an acceptable service to their students. This is clearly not a position that should be allowed to continue. At the present time there are enormous anxieties amongst lecturers about the measures of teaching competence, and the possibility that disciplinary action might be taken against teachers who fall below a minimum standard of competence. I understand and sympathize with these fears, but I do not believe in the long term it does the profession of university lecturer any service to be protective of those who fail to live up to the very high standards undoubtedly set by the majority of their colleagues.

The performance of the individual teacher is only one ingredient in the teaching quality measure of any department or institution. The way in which courses are constructed, and the stimulus that is provided for the student in the demands and progressive nature of the course have quite rightly been a major concern of the validation and course approval processes in the former polytechnics and colleges sector. Many university colleagues have commented that the process of reviewing the experience of a course in its totality would enhance some university procedures. Modularization and credit accumulation and transfer will, of course, throw a very different light on the kinds of questions we are accustomed to ask about 'a course' as an entity in its own right. We shall have to learn to look at the progression routes offered through modules, to ensure that the routes open to individual students do still provide a satisfactory experience in terms of progression and integrity. It cannot be said too often that the real quality of higher education must be measured in terms of what the students know, understand and can do at the end of their higher education experience. These are unquestionably the criteria used by employers and by society at large. They are not ones that we in the higher education system should shirk. Too great an emphasis on measuring input without regard to this output measure has been a fault of the CNAA system in the past. This habit still casts its long shadow over many internal validation and review procedures.

A quality ethos

The overall climate and ethos of an institution is one of the major contribu-
tors to the richness of student experience, far beyond the specific experience
within the classroom contact on an individual course. I do not believe that
higher education is worthy of the name unless the institutions that offer it are
staffed by people who themselves have scholarly activity and interest upper-
most in their own lives. This provides a climate in which students learn a
respect for the pursuit of knowledge, and enlarge for themselves that key
element in human intellect, which is unending curiosity. In a similar way, the
climate of relationships with the working world outside the institutions is an
essential ingredient of the quality of student experience. Students who are
preparing for working life need an understanding of the way in which higher
education teaching and research contributes to the value of the economic life
of their country, and need to develop a sense of pride in their own potential
contribution to that economic life. Only a tiny proportion of graduates, or
even of those who obtain masters degrees, will remain in academic life. An
academic institution which, by its ethos and attitudes, offers no sympathy
with any world other than its own, is failing to provide any sense of identity
with the future lives of a very large proportion of its students.

   Although there is no escaping the fact that the senior management of
an institution bears responsibility for the quality of the whole of its provision, nevertheless senior management alone cannot, by policing-style checks,
balances and monitoring, create quality in the day-to-day life of the students.
It is the lecturer in the workshop, laboratory or classroom who delivers to the
students their experience of higher education. Unless each lecturer accepts
personal responsibility for the quality of service delivered, all the monitoring
and checking in the world will not improve the service. Equally, the lecturer
in day-to-day contact with students can only deliver a high quality service if
those who provide a service to the academic staff in administration, buildings,
canteens and audio-visual services, in turn recognize and accept responsibility
for total quality in what they provide. In other words, quality has to be
'owned' by every member of staff throughout the institution if the service is
to carry any guarantee of reliably high standards.

   The TQM approach now being adopted through many large commercial
and industrial concerns is one that has very direct relevance for the higher
education system. It is one that we are certainly pursuing at my own institution,
South Bank University. It takes a long time: it takes a great deal of painful
heart-searching on the part of every individual member of staff: it takes a
great deal of time spent on training and more training: it takes a willingness
to be open with colleagues and to accept responsibility when things go wrong.
Such a change in the institutional culture can only be produced if senior
management is willing to devolve the responsibility for quality, and along
with it the responsibility for resources and decisions, to give to each individual
a sense of autonomy in the job they do. Responsibility cannot be accepted
unless there is autonomy to be exercised. People cannot be responsible for

decisions over which they have no personal control, nor can they retain any enthusiasm for quality if the circumstances in which they work, and those on whom they depend, fail to deliver them the information, training and tools that they need to perform effectively.

Real devolution of power is not easy: it requires an act of faith and confidence on the part of senior management, which many are understandably reluctant to take. Nevertheless, the climate of overall quality can only be achieved if the process of devolution, retaining control only of those decisions that must be made by senior management, is not only followed but is also seen and understood by all in the institution.

Quality is the great and exciting challenge to higher education in the next decade. It is quality that has to be achieved against a diminishing unit of resource, and at a time that promises to be one of continuous expansion and change. The great universities of the United Kingdom have achieved excellence that is internationally recognized. But they have undoubtedly achieved this against a background of generous funding from government, industry and their ancient benefactors. For the rest of the higher education system, excellence, which is equal but different in nature, must be achieved against a very different financial and resource background. It is incumbent on each institution to define for itself the nature of the excellence it seeks, uninhibited by the models of the past.

I would like to believe that the newly unified system of higher education will achieve excellence in diversity, serving the needs of an increasingly technological and high skilled society, with diverse needs and a diverse population. More than any other single institution in our society, higher education holds the key to our future national prosperity. We cannot afford to delay much longer the provision of a high quality service geared not to the past but to the challenge of the future.

References

1. Perry, Baroness P. (1991) Quality in higher education. In Schuller, T. (ed.) *The Future of Higher Education*. Buckingham, Open University Press.
2. Naisbitt, J. and Aburdene, P. (1989) *Megatrends 2000*. London, Pan Books.

4

Inspecting Quality in the Classroom: An HMI Perspective

Terry Melia

Introduction

The 1992 Further and Higher Education Act brought to an end the role of Her Majesty's Inspectorate in monitoring and evaluating the quality of provision within higher education. The only exception is initial teacher training, which has historically been more tightly regulated by government than other subject areas. The methodology of the Inspectorate shared many features with other agencies responsible for quality control. However, the observation of the student's learning experience in the classroom and the incorporation of judgements of the quality of his/her experience into the overall gradings used to describe the quality of provision in an inspected institution was a feature unique to the Inspectorate.

The remit of the Inspectorate was restricted to one side of the binary line: the polytechnics and colleges of higher education. Access to the traditional universities was limited to departments responsible for initial teacher training. Even here, access was by invitation only. The role of the Inspectorate was always controversial. It became even more so when the PCFC experimented with linking quality judgements to funding decisions. This chapter therefore marks the demise of a major 'stakeholder' in higher education and the end of a particular approach to and a method of quality control.

Quality is an elusive concept. All claim to recognize it but few can adequately describe what they mean by it, much less define and measure it.

In preparing this chapter, I set myself three tasks. These are:

1. To explain what I understand by the terms quality and standards.
2. To indicate how Her Majesty's Inspectorate (HMI) evaluated standards of learning and the quality of the student experience.
3. To outline how HMI judgements on the quality of provision at the course/department/faculty/institutional levels were used to inform policy and funding decisions.

Quality and standards

If quality in education is difficult to define, we can say that it is dependent on many important factors. It is to do with the pursuit of scholarship through teaching, research or study. It is to do with a sense of order and structure; the good lecture has been carefully plotted and organized. It is to do with maximum student engagement; in the good lecture, the students' attention is fully held and their enthusiasm and interest sustained. It is to do with achievement; in the good lesson the students leave enriched, having been set, and having achieved, appropriate standards. Quality is to do with all that which supports teaching and learning. There is quality in terms of teaching; the good teacher has up-to-date knowledge of his/her subject, is enthusiastic about it, understands how people learn, has attractive personal character-istics, uses a variety of teaching methods and has high expectations of the students. There is quality in terms of accommodation; the provision of suitable classrooms, workshops and laboratories that are conducive to learning. There is quality in terms of equipment and resources; the provision of well designed teaching and learning aids and a library that is well resourced, adequately staffed and well used. Yet, the starting point in the quest for quality must be the actual learning process. It is sometimes possible to achieve good practice in poor accommodation and with poor resources. Ironically, it is also possible for poor or even bad teaching or learning to occur in excellent accommoda-tion and for it to involve good resources. Here the plot thickens, for the resources, though good in themselves, have little value in a context where they are misapplied. This, in turn, leads to two important conclusions: first, that quality is concerned with fitness for purpose; second, a chief prerequisite for quality is the identification of clear and appropriate objectives at the institutional, departmental and course levels.

On the face of it, the concept of standards is more straightforward than that of quality. In fact we can even attempt a definition along the lines that standards refer to levels of achievement against which performance can be assessed. Such a definition implies that standards are measurable. But we then need to pose the question: 'Measurable against what?' – does this imply measuring performance against some *absolute* standard, academic criteria? (and what about values?). Again, fitness for purpose must be the yardstick against which we judge standards at all levels of education. Let me illustrate this with an example from higher education. Britain, along with many other countries, is striving to move from an elite to a mass system of higher education. It is evident that no single approach to expansion would be appropriate. We need a wide variety of institutions offering a range of subjects and courses at dif-ferent levels, in the full-time and part-time modes and at different costs. In such a higher education system, academic standards must be appropriate to both the students and their programmes of study. We must recognize that the criteria applied to the traditional elite higher education provision is not an appropriate yardstick against which all higher education institutions, or the programmes of study they offer, can be judged. Research and scholarship are particularly relevant in this connection. The research and scholarship needs of those teaching in a mass higher education system are very different from those teaching in an elite system.

The evaluation of quality

Quality assurance, quality control and inspection are significant aspects of the assessment, maintenance and enhancement of quality. Quality assurance provides users of the higher education system with a guarantee that institutions, courses and graduates meet certain standards. Quality control embraces the methods used to maintain and enhance quality. Inspection is concerned with standards of learning and is based on the direct observation of students and their teachers at work. It involves professional judgement, which is collective rather than individual, and draws on a knowledge of national as well as regional and local standards.

The main guardians of standards and quality are the higher education institutions themselves. They, like others, including inspectors, the examining and validating bodies, the professional bodies and the Higher Education Quality Council (HEQC) are engaged in the evaluation of higher education provision.

This chapter focuses on the work of Her Majesty's Inspectorate, to describe the work of the Inspectors and the framework within which they made their judgements and assessments.

Inspection of higher education

On the basis of inspection, HMI's role was to assess standards and trends, identify and disseminate good practice and provide advice and assistance.

There were four principal objectives of HMI inspection activity as carried out in higher education. First, inspection provided Ministers and Department of Education and Science officials with independent professional advice on the state of higher education. The second objective was to provide quality and other advice to the Polytechnics and Colleges Funding Council (PCFC) and others responsible for operating the system and to monitor PCFC's performance. Third, HMI aimed to identify and disseminate good practice through reports, conferences and courses. Fourth, Inspectors monitored and reported on:

1. Institutional quality and effectiveness.
2. The response of the higher education service to access policies.
3. The impact of the research and enterprise initiatives on higher education.
4. The impact of funding policies in higher education on:
   (a) the quality of teaching and learning;
   (b) the capital building and equipment stock;

    (c) the quality of continuing education and training and its success in
        updating the workforce;

    (d) access and participation.

5. Quality control and the work of the Council for National Academic Awards
   (CNAA) and the Business and Technician Education Council (BTEC)
   and others.

6. The development of performance indicators.

In latter years there was extensive inspection of higher education by HMI
and few institutions escaped some form of HMI scrutiny.

    What did Her Majesty's Inspectorate do? HMI gathered evidence through
the direct observation and evaluation of what happened in educational institutions. There were six strands to our inspection strategy in higher education:

1. Inspections of institutional quality in polytechnics and other colleges of
   higher education.

2. Short inspections of specialist subjects or areas of work in PCFC and LEA
   institutions.

3. Reviews of the major areas of specialist provision in the polytechnics and
   colleges.

4. Development of a grading scale allowing HMI to compare quality both
   across the sector and for the sector as a whole in order to inform funding
   policies as well as the distribution of funds.

5. The development of capital equipment models to inform and evaluate
   capital equipment bids for the PCFC sector.

6. Inspection surveys focusing on particular topics, for example, access and
   the use of performance indicators.

Latterly there was a heavy emphasis on the inspection of specialist subject
areas because it was this that underpinned HMI advice to PCFC in relation
to the quality judgements which impacted on funding decisions.

    HMI inspection reports were published and copies of reports on institu-
tions were available free of charge. In addition, we also sold publications that
dealt with broader issues, for example, *The English Polytechnics* and the series
Higher Education in the Polytechnics and Colleges.

Advice to the funding council

A controversial aspect of HMI's work in latter years was its role in relation
to the Polytechnics and Colleges Funding Council. When the PCFC was
established, the Secretary of State asked the Inspectorate to give whatever
help it could to the new body. The Inspectorate was the main source of
advice to the PCFC on quality in several different ways. Individual inspectors
served as assessors to programme advisory groups. They assisted in the process
of adjudicating claims by institutions of outstanding quality in respect of

specific areas of their provision. They also contributed to the debate about evaluation by publication of criteria used by HMI for the assessment of quality.

Her Majesty's Inspectorate also assisted the PCFC with specific tasks, for example, with advice on membership of its advisory committees and working groups; advice on funding methodology, especially as regards the definition of programme areas, and the allocation of funds for capital equipment. Advice was also produced through assessors and papers to various PCFC groups established to look at a wide range of topics including:

- teaching quality;
- performance indicators;
- research;
- statistical information;
- music conservatoires;
- mergers and redesignation of institutions as polytechnics.

The inspection process

Our prime concern, as inspectors, was with standards of learning. Our interest in organization and management, resources, quality control arrangements and even the teaching itself derived from the impact these had upon standards of learning. For example, certain sorts of equipment are necessary to ensure appropriate standards of learning in certain aspects of science, engineering or computing. We were not so much interested in the equipment *per se* but its role in facilitating learning. The evaluation of learning was our central purpose. It was the role of HMI to report upon the quality of the education as offered throughout the schools and colleges of the land. The basis of our judgements was often in comparison. HMI inspectors were privileged to see a wide range of provision. We saw some educational practice that was excellent, some that was poor and some somewhere in between. To some extent, we redefined quality as we went.

In order to judge the quality and effectiveness of an area of work or of a course, we examined first its aims and objectives. We then attempted to assess whether or not the organization and management, resources and range and appropriateness of provision allowed these aims and objectives to be effectively achieved. Then, and only then, did we judge whether the aims and outcomes compared with those of similar courses or areas of work and whether they were appropriate.

In a typical inspection, Inspectors sought to evaluate:

- aims and objectives;
- organization and management;
- appropriateness of resources;
- range and appropriateness of provision;
- teaching and learning;

- outcomes;
- quality control and assurance arrangements.

Assessing and rating quality

The criteria used by the Inspectorate to assess the quality of provision in higher education were set out in the HMI paper *In Pursuit of Quality: An HMI View*.[1] In the light of the criteria identified in this paper, five broad grade descriptors were used to summarize our findings:

1. Generally good, or with many outstanding features or with many good features.
2. Some good features and no major shortcomings.
3. Sound, with no significant extremes or good features balanced by shortcomings.
4. Some shortcomings in important areas.
5. Many shortcomings, generally poor.

The attraction of grades or ratings scales are considerable. They facilitate retrieval and analysis as well as improving the validity of generalizations based on a large number of independent judgements. When grades are reported, the institutions inspected and the readers of published reports are faced with clearer messages about the quality of educational provision and response and are therefore less likely to misinterpret evaluations. Furthermore, during inspections the use of a rating scale encouraged individual inspectors to focus sharply on qualitative judgements and helped a team to come to better collective judgements.

However, there are difficulties and potential dangers in the use of rating scales. We were aware of these and believed that we developed appropriate techniques based on sound principles and procedures. In essence, HMI considered the implications of producing grades that combine different kinds of judgements. Many of the features that HMI were required to rate are multi-faceted. We also needed to consider the effect of combining grades that were awarded by different inspectors. This raised the problem of the reliability of different individuals engaged in the rating exercise (inter-rater reliability). We were aware of the need to make judgements that took account of specific circumstances, and the desirability of using relative rather than absolute criteria. We also recognized the possibility that HMI grades, when aggregated, might tend towards a norm-referenced distribution, and the possibility that strong encouragement to grade a wide range of features, as routine practice, might induce inspectors to base some of their judgements on very limited evidence.

HMI strived to ensure that their use of grades did not give a spurious impression of precision, which did not stand up to close critical scrutiny. The right policy is not to abandon the use of rating scales but to be cautious in their application, to ensure that they are used appropriately and that the grades awarded are correctly analysed. It is important to distinguish between the different uses of such scales, in particular between:

1. Their use as part of the process of sharpening evaluation and reporting, for example by helping focus on variations in quality and to reach sound collective judgements.
2. Their use to facilitate retrieval of information.
3. Their use as data for analysis and generalization.

Many have questioned whether grades awarded to individual courses, departments or institutions should be made public. But it is the mood of the times with which we must learn to live. However, when grades are subjected to an analysis that is subsequently reported it may be necessary to give an account of the procedures used and a summary of the distribution of grades, in order to show how particular conclusions have been reached. In these cases tight guidelines are required, not least to ensure that adequate attention is given to inter-rater reliability and procedures for sampling. Given that most ratings contain component and overall judgements, it is important to retain both aspects for subsequent analysis. HMI was guided by the key principles that the scales should be as simple as possible. Complex judgements involving trade-offs should be avoided, and the basic data should be retained to allow further analyses. When reports included generalizations based on analyses of grades, care was taken to ensure that the text helped readers to interpret the findings correctly.

It was a measure of the success that HMI achieved in developing rating scales that these were widely accepted in the PCFC sector for funding purposes. The report of the PCFC Committee of Enquiry into Performance Indicators[2] recommended that the HMI descriptors might usefully be adapted to provide the key macro-indicators of the health and quality of courses on each of PCFC's nine programmes, and that they should be used to support the PCFC annual bid for funds.

Conclusion

Evaluation of any type, be it inspection, validation or auditing, has no value if it is carried out without any account being taken of the policy framework and context within which an aspect of education is being conducted. Nor is it sufficient to base an evaluation of higher education provision on examination of documents and the holding of discussions. It is essential to observe what is going on, to look into what is happening, and to assess the appropriateness and use of the resources. It is vital always to bear in mind the need to help both teachers and students so as to ensure that the students receive as good an education as possible. In this respect, inspection, which offers constructive criticism, is a powerful tool supporting quality improvement as well as the maintenance of standards.

References

1. HMI (1989) In pursuit of quality: an HMI view. In *Quality in Higher Education*. Report on the HMI conference at Heythrop Park 16–18 June 1989, unpublished proceedings.
2. PCFC (1990) *Performance Indicators*. (Report of a Committee of Enquiry, chaired by A. Morris.) London, PCFC.

5

Quality Audit in the Universities

Carole Webb

Introduction

The new Academic Audit Unit (AAU) established by the Committee of Vice-Chancellors and Principals (CVCP) formally came into operation in 1990. Within two years the Unit had been subsumed into a larger organization with a wider remit, and covering the whole of the higher education system. In July 1992, following the changes made in the landscape of the higher education system by the Further and Higher Education Act, the Higher Education Quality Council (HEQC) formally came into being to serve as a prime focus for activity concerned with maintaining and enhancing quality. The journey charted by quality audit between 1990 and 1992 was interesting and taxing; academic auditors, at least for the 'old' universities (i.e. those that carried the title before the 1992 Act) were developing and implementing an untried method for the external review of quality assurance (itself still a relatively new term), whilst the higher education system as a whole was being buffeted by storms, swirls and harbingers of change, which would test even the most well-established systems and procedures for maintaining quality. In the event, the absorption of the Academic Audit Unit into the Division of Quality Audit (DQA) of the HEQC, and the support given to the Council by old and new universities (and other institutions of higher education in the UK) reflected the extent to which the 'old' universities had come to accept external quality audit as an appropriate and worthwhile activity, and the expectation that it was capable of further adaptation and refinement to take into account the different traditions, and still developing quality cultures, of the 'new' universities.

Quality and quality audit

The very titles of both the Academic Audit Unit and the Division of Quality Audit have boldly embraced words and concepts that continue to be the subject of much controversy, both within and outside higher education. 'Audit' and 'quality' evoke expectations about reliability, probity, standards and excellence, which have led to much debate about whether either, or both, terms are applicable to higher education, where the prevailing professional and organizational ethos has been largely inimical to practices and procedures commonplace in other sectors. The term 'audit' was suggested by Professor Stewart Sutherland, Vice-Chancellor of the University of London and chairman of the CVCP's Academic Standards Group and of the Management Board of the Academic Audit Unit between 1990 and 1992, partly in order to distinguish academic audit from other kinds of peer review exercises, and partly to hint at the intended methodology that would characterize this form of external academic review. Academic audit would seek to borrow and adapt some techniques from financial audit, such as the scrutiny of an institution's documented procedures and practices, the examination of these in operation through detailed inquiries and discussions with staff (and students), and the sampling of a wide range of activity and evidence, to establish and test the robustness and effectiveness of academic quality assurance. The analogy with financial audit was known to be far from perfect; it was not meant to imply that a university's teaching and learning activities are comparable with a company's balance sheet, or that they are susceptible to similar forms of analysis. Indeed, the starting point for an academic audit was, and remains, an institution's stated aims and objectives and its stated means of assuring the quality, in particular, of its activities associated with teaching and learning. This approach has enjoined audit teams to bring an open, non-prescriptive perspective to each institutional audit and to review arrangements for quality assurance agnostically, rather than from a conviction that a given set of procedures or an approach must be right, irrespective of the institutional context or an institution's declared aims and objectives.

Definitions of quality, which carry any degree of precision or general acceptance within and outside higher education, have proved hard, if not impossible, to find. From the outset, the AAU sought to avoid the definitional game in the belief that it was unlikely to lead to any worthwhile result, and that it was likely to inhibit rather than assist the Unit's task of focusing on how institutions assured the quality of the whole range of their teaching and learning provision. UK universities, by virtue of their charters, statutes and powers defined by Acts of Parliament, set their own standards and determine how quality will be defined in their own terms. The notion of a single 'gold standard', applied to the first degree, is neither well-founded nor helpful when applied to the range, diversity and complexity of the teaching and learning offered in higher education institutions. Such institutions share a number of common objectives, particularly in respect to their teaching function, perhaps less so in research. But there are also a number of very discernible differences, which, increasingly, mission statements and publicly-declared objectives are seeking to communicate to wider audiences. Some of these differences have a direct bearing on the character and educational ethos of an institution, and are intended to be reflected in the educational experience offered to students. The AAU, therefore, sought to ask of institutions not 'why are you not doing this in this way?' but 'what are you doing, why, to what effect, and how do you know that what you are doing (to promote and enhance quality) works?' The Unit's successor, the Division of Quality Audit, faced with the challenging task of preparing to audit nearly 100 degree-awarding institutions, has sought fully to acknowledge institutional and mission diversity and, at the same time, to maintain overall a fair and even-handed approach to each audit. It is not in the business of matching institutions with a pre-ordained template. To serve as a guide to its teams and to convey the purpose and flavour of its approach, the Division has sought to incorporate the definition offered in the British Standard 7229 *Quality Systems Auditing*[1] into its work:

> Quality audit is a systematic and independent examination to determine whether quality activities and related results comply with planned arrangements and whether these arrangements are implemented effectively and are suitable to achieve objectives.

Thus, an academic quality audit will not concern itself with the validity of an institution's objectives but with the ways in which that institution manages those aspects of its work that impinge on quality. It will not be concerned directly with academic standards (in the sense of their verification in subject or programme areas) but with how an institution satisfies itself that these are being achieved. Quality audits are, therefore, quite distinct, and wholly different in purpose and rationale, from inspections, programme validation and approval or assessment exercises undertaken by HMI and CNAA in the past, by professional and accrediting bodies, or, in the future, by the funding councils. A fundamental premise of the AAU, carried into the work of the DQA, is that academic quality will be most effectively safeguarded, and is more likely to be enhanced, where institutions are responsible for their quality assurance and for determining their own arrangements for this purpose. Audit is intentionally reticent about prescribing practices and advocating uniformity; its concern is with what is done, whether this is demonstrably effective and, if it can be shown to be so, making that knowledge available to others.

If the search for a generally agreed definition of quality in higher education is proving to be a chimera, definitions of quality in respect of teaching and of students' learning (expressed, in the latter case, in terms of a student's acquisition of skills and knowledge derived from individual and group learning experience) are equally elusive. The AAU quickly learned that its remit to examine the effectiveness of systems and procedures for maintaining and enhancing teaching and learning was made much more difficult by the relative paucity of knowledge on what constitutes good teaching, and the limited circulation of what is known, amongst teachers and students in higher education.[2] This relative lack of knowledge (in comparison with, for example, the knowledge of research techniques), and the sense amongst many academics that possession of such knowledge (and, even more, the sharing of it with others) was deemed, if anything, to count against promotion because it might be seen to indicate a weak or insufficient commitment to research, has helped to shape the audit process. Quality audit is concerned with purposeful inquiry, not with absolute judgement. This is not to say that audit teams have found the task of quality audit too daunting, or the context of each audit inquiry too institutionally idiosyncratic, to generate findings of general interest to the higher education sector, or, indeed to a wider community. The list of such findings referred to by the AAU's Director, in his first Annual Report, opened up some major areas of common concern and interest where further consideration and action were needed.[3] These included, for example, issues concerning the efficacy of the external examiner system and an urgent need to find ways of identifying and rewarding good teaching, both being fundamental to the maintenance and enhancement of standards in the UK system of higher education.

The CVCP Academic Audit Unit

In a chronological sense, the history of the Academic Audit Unit covers the short period between 1989 and 1992, although the Unit built upon CVCP-initiated inquiries begun in the 1980s, and its work has been substantially incorporated into the remit and programme of the Division of Quality Audit from 1992 onwards. Until the early 1980s, academic standards in universities were seen to be very largely the business of the universities themselves. Not only did university charters enshrine the principle of university autonomy, but the professional academic culture nurtured a sense of pride in and adherence to the principle of individual excellence, which has proved strongly resistant to the opening up of certain fundamental areas, such as the quality of university teaching and student learning to external, or even to internal, scrutiny and review. However, from the early 1980s, and following the 1979 Conservative Government's determination to expose the whole range of publicly-funded services to greater scrutiny in order to secure more effective accountability for, and efficiency in, public expenditure, the universities found themselves needing to defend not only their standards and quality, but the means by which these were determined institutionally, and with reference to wider national economic goals. Following the Jarratt Report's[4] study of university policy, decision-making and resource allocation procedures the CVCPs instigated a more detailed inquiry into university policy and practice in relation to the setting and maintaining of academic standards. The work of the CVCP Reynolds Committee (chaired by Professor Philip Reynolds, then Vice-Chancellor of Lancaster University) led to a wide-ranging report published in 1986,[5] to two further follow-up reports based on questionnaires returned by universities and to the development of codes of practice in certain key areas such as external examiners, postgraduate supervision and provision for appeals by research degree students. The codes were accompanied by detailed statements offering guidance to universities on how they might develop or improve procedures to secure standards in the design and monitoring of student programmes of study. Whilst the initial inquiries and follow-up work (subsequently taken over by the CVCP's Academic Standards Group, under the chairmanship of Professor Stewart Sutherland), succeeded in putting standards and academic quality on to the collective university agenda, it did not stem the flow of questioning and criticism of the ability of universities to regulate their own academic affairs. Such questioning was particularly pointed and challenging when reference was made by critics, and by champions of the other publicly-funded segment of higher education, to the polytechnics' and colleges' experience of external validation and review through the Council for National Academic Awards. The universities responded to what was clearly seen as a challenge to their autonomy and organizational robustness in terms of setting and maintaining academic standards, and at the suggestion of the Academic Standards Group, by agreeing to establish the Academic Audit Unit with a brief to undertake detailed audits of individual universities. Plans for the Unit were drawn up in 1990 and it came into operation from October 1990 as a Unit wholly owned and financed (through an additional levy on universities administered by CVCP) by the universities.

From the outset, the Unit was seen as having both an auditing function and, through the dissemination of examples of good practice, a developmental role in relation to university policy and practice. The Unit's terms of reference referred to both aspects:

1. To consider and review the universities' mechanisms for monitoring and promoting the academic standards necessary for achieving their stated aims and objectives.
2. To comment on the extent to which procedures in place in individual universities reflect best practice in maintaining quality and are applied in practice.
3. To identify and commend to universities good practice in regard to the maintenance of academic standards at the national level.
4. To keep under review nationally the role of the external examiner system.

The starting point and benchmark for good practice were the CVCP's codes of practice. These touched on four broad areas, which were seen as central to the maintenance and enhancement of standards and where there was a reasonable presumption (not least from work of the Academic Standards Group) that institutions would have procedures and mechanisms in place. The four areas were listed and amplified (in an indicative list of questions) in a checklist for the use of auditors. Its purpose was not to limit audit teams to a box-ticking exercise, but to give a consistent shape and coverage to each audit, and to indicate what range of mechanisms and procedures at all levels in an institution might have a bearing on its capacity to undertake effective quality assurance. The four broad areas included in the checklist were:

1. Quality assurance in the provision and design of programmes and courses.
2. Quality assurance in teaching, learning and communication (between staff and students and throughout the institution).

3. Quality assurance in relation to academic staff.
4. Quality assurance in relation to feedback from external examiners, students and external bodies (including employers).

The checklist was incorporated into the *Notes for Guidance for Auditors* which, although not formally published and conceived primarily as a working document for the auditors themselves, was nevertheless circulated widely to institutions and to other interested parties. To a greater or lesser extent, it soon came to be regarded as a starting point for many an internal informal audit to prepare an institution for the visit of an external audit team.

One of the key features of the Audit Unit's approach was the prominence given to peer review as the basis of external audit. The Unit was not to be an officer-led body. Its full-time staffing establishment of a Director, Deputy Director and Unit Administrator was deliberately very small; the Unit's headquarters in Birmingham serving as a central co-ordinating point and meeting venue for audit teams and the twice-yearly meetings of auditors. The latter provide an opportunity for auditors to exchange information and experience, and to review audit methodology in the light of feedback and reflection upon current audit practice. The burden of audit falls on the auditors themselves. Four groups of auditors (totalling 51 in all) were recruited by the Audit Unit between 1990 and 1992 from an extensive list of nominees submitted by vice-chancellors at the request of the Unit. The requirements of potential auditors were that individuals should be active in teaching, have recognized standing in their subject and have experience of and an interest in academic quality assurance by involvement in relevant activities, either within or outside the university (for example through involvement with a professional or accrediting body). In selecting individual auditors the Unit sought to achieve a subject balance that would, in the broadest terms, reflect the range of disciplines offered in universities, and an appropriate mix of individuals from different parts of the UK and from different types of university institutions. Auditors were invited to serve part-time with the Unit, initially seconded for up to the equivalent of 20 per cent of their time and paid a modest fee (calculated as a daily rate) for their work. Each auditor was asked to be prepared to undertake up to four institutional audits per year, and to complete a three-stage induction programme, organized by the Unit's Directorate (initially in collaboration with the University's Staff Development and Training Unit) as an essential precursor to becoming a member of an audit team. Audit teams normally consist of three auditors, together with an audit secretary, the latter recruited for each audit from middle-grade administrators nominated from universities at the request of the Unit. Although the concept of audit secretaries emerged in an *ad hoc* way as a means of providing a much-needed resource for audit teams, particularly in the keeping of a systematic record of the audit visit discussions that provide much of the raw material from which auditors compile their report, audit secretaries have proved to be a potent source of staff development, both for the individuals themselves and for their institutions.

The audit process

In devising an audit methodology, the Unit, with the support of its Management Board, whose members were drawn from representative heads of universities in membership of the CVCP and individuals from related outside organizations and industry, sought to develop a style and pattern of activity consistent with its objective of identifying and testing systems and procedures in operation. The Unit established a tripartite audit process consisting of a *briefing* stage, at which the university's briefing for the audit team on its quality assurance processes can be examined in detail, followed by an audit *visit* so that the university's claimed procedures and processes can be examined *in situ*, and concluding with the team's *report* of the audit. The whole process has normally taken about nine months, with the period from the delivery of the initial briefing documentation to the delivery of the draft report to the university vice-chancellor lasting, normally, about 12 to 14 weeks.

Whilst the audit visit has been, perhaps, the most visible stage of the process, the audit team begins to form its view, and formulate its detailed inquiries at the briefing stage in the light of the briefing documentation it receives. This can be very weighty and substantial, or relatively concise and thematically presented, although the experience of the Audit Unit was that many universities appear to have set value by weight and volume. The Unit's guidance on briefing documentation has been cast in permissive language, in the belief that, at least in the first audit cycle, it was appropriate to suggest to institutions that they 'tell their story' of quality assurance in their own terms. The Unit's expectation has been that briefing material would fall, broadly, into three categories: examples of formal publications such as annual reports, prospectuses and calendars; policy, procedural and regulatory material already in existence and examples illustrative of procedures in operation, such as external examiners' reports, staff development programmes, monitoring and review papers relating to current programmes of study and minutes of bodies directly responsible for quality assurance. The ease, or otherwise, with which an institution can assemble such material may serve as a rough indicator of its stage of development in quality assurance terms, whilst allowing for some scepticism that documented procedures necessarily constitute a fair and reliable measure of an institution's preparedness to commit itself to purposeful quality assurance.

Each audit team has approximately one month to digest the briefing material and to prepare for a meeting at which its audit agenda must be identified and a programme of meetings with staff and students devised. The team's briefing meeting is important, not merely for the exchange of views and impressions, but also as an opportunity for the team's working method to be established in some detail. As audit teams have been formed and re-formed by the Unit's Directorate, auditors find themselves working intensely hard and intensively with most of their colleagues. Chairing skills, styles of inquiry and specific information-eliciting strategies devised by auditors (such as the tracking of decision-making and its outcome through audit trails, and the matching of responses from one group with those of others on the same topic) need to be identified and responsibilities assigned. The team may also require some additional information from the university, or clarification of points made in the briefing papers. Any such requests are normally made to allow at least one month for a response from the institution before the audit visit commences.

The audit visit, normally consisting of three days of meetings and discussions with staff and students (for the most part selected by the audit team or by the university to accord with the request of the team to see particular groupings) is the most concentrated stage of the audit process. It is also liable to be misunderstood, or its significance unduly heightened by an institution whose staff may be concerned that colleagues 'do not perform well on the day', or even that the team, through its questioning and inquiry, might expose differences of view and levels of awareness. There is no escaping a certain amount of artificiality and advanced preparedness for audit visits; auditors, as academic peers, do not have unlimited availability, and if visits are to succeed in their primary aim of allowing the team to explore mechanisms and procedures described in the university's briefing papers, meetings with staff and students need to be arranged in good time. Audit teams will seek to keep their intrusion into the life of the university to a minimum by programming meetings to a tight timetable that is resolutely maintained, and by meeting either individuals or small groups to ensure that participants' time is not wasted. An audit team, through its programme and its agenda, will be seeking to establish both a general understanding of institutional mechanisms and procedures, and whether, in operation, they are serving the declared aims and objectives of the university. Teams may identify a number of themes to be pursued with groupings at different levels across a range of academic areas, such as the design of new programmes, programme review and mechanisms for monitoring student progress or for matching assessment strategies with programme objectives. They may also, or in preference, choose to slice the 'system' vertically, by selecting two or three departments, or programmes, that cut across departmental boundaries and explore the operation of procedures in these areas over a defined period of time. However a team decides to design its programme, it will seek to ensure that its audit inquiries are probing all aspects of an institution's approach to quality assurance, and at each identifiable level in that institution.

Following the visit the team, whose responsibility it is to prepare the first draft, will begin work immediately on the written report, often extending the visit to ensure that members of the team, in conjunction with the audit secretary (who will have already provided the team with summaries of each day's discussions and will provide a fuller record within a week or so of the end of the visit), can agree the main findings and assign the remaining drafting tasks. Draft reports come into the Directorate for editing to ensure consistency across all audit reports and are sent to vice-chancellors for correction of factual errors and comment on any judgements that appear to be based on misconceptions. The final audit report should be with the institution some 10 to 12 weeks after the audit visit. Audit reports are intended to provide a full and fair account of a university's approach to quality assurance and its systems and procedures in operation. They also contain examples of good practice which, in the team's view, are worthy of record not merely for the institution in question, but for the attention of others. Audit teams will also record, in the form of recommendations, areas that the university may wish to consider, or reconsider, in the light of the team's investigations. In the early period of the CVCP Academic Audit Unit's existence much attention was paid to the possible tone and the public availability of audit reports. From the outset the Unit sought to avoid a strident or bellicose tone, believing not merely that this would be likely to elicit defensive reactions from institutions and thereby draw attention away from the purpose of improving and enhancing quality assurance, but that the essentially voluntary principle associated with external academic audit required that reports engage with, and not contest, universities' concerns for quality. The agreement of universities to the establishment of the AAU included the decision that the Unit would not publish audit reports but that each university would decide whether to put its report in the public domain. In the event, and excluding the reports of the pilot audits (most of which were, in fact, made available by the universities concerned), almost all universities have chosen to make their audit reports available, mostly on request; some have given them immediate and wide circulation through re-production in university newsletters and comparable publications.

Audit findings

At the time of writing, 27 audits had been completed from the audit pro-gramme originally established by the AAU for the university sector as it existed prior to the 1992 Further and Higher Education Act. That programme had been planned to allow for the completion of audits of all universities by December 1993. The remaining audits (which will be completed under the aegis of the Higher Education Quality Council) include completion of the audit of the University of London, involving over 20 visits to this federal University and its component schools and colleges (some of which are larger than other universities), and separate audits of universities that validate courses offered by other colleges and institutions leading to university awards. By September 1992, and some 18 months since the first pilot audit got under way, the audit process had been tested in a variety of university contexts, it had devised ways of looking at a range of systems and procedures, audits had been completed of a highly specialized university college (the University of Wales College of Medicine) and of a large, ancient and collegiate institution (the University of Cambridge). The five pilot audits were a useful period of apprenticeship for the Audit Unit. They enabled judgements to be made at an early stage on whether the audit method was soundly based, whether it would prove to be unduly burdensome on institutions, and whether this kind of inquiry could generate useful information for individual universities and higher education more generally. A number of changes were made to the method at this stage in the light of university feedback from the pilots. Continuing feedback from auditors and institutions has proved a vital source of intelligence as the audit process has further developed. In a few cases, universities have passed on their own findings on the impact of the audit visit on their own institution (gleaned from variously arranged forms of debriefing of staff and students, including 'exit polling') to the Unit.[6]

It was easy and tempting in the period after the audit schedule was well under way to take the signs of reasonably wide acceptance, or tolerance, of audit teams and audit procedures as an indication that greater attention was being paid to assuring academic standards and to enhancing the quality of the academic experience on offer to students in universities. It quickly became apparent that the very establishment of the Unit had caused a rethink, or a speeding up of thinking, and action in relation to quality assurance. Perhaps not unnaturally, much of this had to do with the perceived imminence of an audit visit, or the desirability of providing a coherent account of systems and procedures in advance of a visit. One of the main findings referred to in the Director's first Annual Report on the Unit was of the volume of activity recorded across the university system concerned with matters such as the assembly and collation of information on procedures and practices, the establishment of teaching quality committees, clearer guidance for external examiners and improved reporting procedures, and the beginning of a discussion on the identification of, and reward for, good teaching. However, in the words of one of the auditors who subsequently joined the full-time staff on secondment from his university, 'what is important is not the audit itself, but what it causes to happen'. Setting aside the immediate (positive and negative) effects on an institution of its senior officers requiring papers, flow charts and answers to questions in order to construct briefing documentation for an external group, the contribution and usefulness of academic audit can only be judged by whether quality is improved and enhanced. The likelihood that one university audit is going to have a dramatic effect on that institution is low, but the accumulation of information from the first 'mapping' of university systems and procedures for quality assurance in operation, and its dissemination across the higher education sector, are likely to raise awareness and cause staff and students to consider whether current provision is as good as it can be.

The Director's first Annual Report[7] provided an opportunity to attempt an initial stock-taking of findings and suggested good practice at a mid-point in the audit schedule. Under six broad headings (course design and monitoring, innovation in teaching and learning, staff development and training, rewarding good teaching, feedback and the external examiner system) comment was offered that drew directly on the detailed findings of audit teams, citing examples where universities appeared to be pioneering new approaches, or where the absence of procedures or differing perceptions of their intent (as, for example, in the area of staff promotion and reward for good teaching) suggested that stated university objectives were unlikely to be fully realized. The Audit Unit's remit to cite good practice that might be capable of adoption or adaptation elsewhere was reflected in the Annual Report's inclusion of an appendix, provided, at the Unit's request, by the University of Southampton, describing its approach to departmental review. The intention was not to prescribe this procedure in its entirety for use elsewhere, but to offer it as a good example of an approach that had been particularly well-thought out, piloted and amended over time, had attracted active support from staff and had yielded results.

From AAU to quality audit and the HEQC

The publication in May 1991 of the Government White Paper *Higher Education: A New Framework*,[8] and the subsequent passing of the Further and Higher Education Act, brought major changes to the framework of the higher education sector, with direct consequences for the development of academic audit. This is not the place to record the discussion and wide-ranging issues that accompanied both the White Paper's publication and the passage of the legislation through both Houses of Parliament. One of the main objectives of the legislation was the designation of nearly 40 new universities by the granting of degree-awarding powers to the ex-polytechnics and the creation of a single higher education sector to replace the sector, divided in so many ways, by the old binary line. The new single sector would be subject to a common form of external 'quality audit'. It was the Government's hope, and the higher education institutions' determination, that quality audit would be undertaken through a structure 'owned' by the institutions themselves. (The 1992 Act contains reserve powers to be exercised by the Secretary of State in the event that institutions either refuse or fail to put in place adequate quality assurance mechanisms monitored by external audit.) The outcome of intense discussions involving the representative bodies for institutions of higher education (the Committee of Vice-Chancellors and Principals, the Committee of Directors of Polytechnics, the Standing Committee of Principals and the Scottish Centrally Funded Colleges) was the creation of a single quality body for all UK institutions: the Higher Education Quality Council (HEQC). The Council has a brief for academic quality that incorporates both audit/assurance and research/development dimensions, and is intended to build upon the practices established by the AAU and the experience exemplified in the CNAA approach to quality assurance in the polytechnics and colleges. The Council has been structured into three Divisions, Quality Audit, Credit and Access, and Quality Enhancement.

From September 1992 the work of the AAU was absorbed into the Division of Quality Audit, the complement of full-time staff expanding to meet the needs of an audit schedule that is likely to cover well over 200 institutions. The intention, nevertheless, is to keep the Division small and to maintain the characteristic of a small central unit supporting and co-ordinating a changing body of seconded auditors. All institutions in membership of the HEQC will be subject to external audit, probably on a three-year cycle, by the Division; other HE institutions not in membership of HEQC may request an external audit by the Division. The remit of the DQA is broadly similar to that of the AAU in respect of the focus and scope of audit. One new area has been added (and there will be some further 'unpacking' of the four broad areas of programme design and review, teaching and learning, staffing and feedback mechanisms so that, for example, greater attention can be paid to assessment and student classification practices, and to accommodate academic provision 'off-campus', such as franchising). Audit teams will be asked to look at quality assurance measures in respect of an institution's promotional material covering its academic provision, and the extent to which such material corresponds accurately with current practice.

Some of the intensity of the preliminary discussions that preceded the creation of the HEQC stemmed from the anxiety of the ex-polytechnics that their own maturation in terms of quality assurance should not be underestimated, nor their experience ignored in the application of external audit to the whole higher education sector. From a quality systems point of view, the structures and approach of the ex-polytechnics (reflecting differences in styles of management and oversight of academic affairs) have, characteristically, been more centralized and, in many cases, more thoroughly documented than has been generally true in the universities. External audit will need to be sensitive to such differences, by continuing to combine purposeful inquiry with peer group discussion, drawing in and upon the full range of experiences and approaches manifest in the sector. The established practice of involving external expertise in the development and review of academic activity in the 'new' universities is but one area where policy and practice can be considered to the benefit of the sector as a whole.

The need to be alert to change and improvement has been ever-present in the short history of the Academic Audit Unit. As the number of completed audits has grown, and the number of auditors increased from the initial group of 14 to nearly 70 (including the first group recruited by the Division under the aegis of the HEQC, more than half of whom come from the 'new' degree-awarding institutions) so the opportunity for incorporating ideas and experimenting with new ways has been seized. Several significant changes have already been made in the light of auditors' suggestions and feedback; perhaps the most important has been an extension to the auditors' induction programme to allow each new auditor to observe part of an audit visit before he/she becomes fully fledged to take part in an audit. The Division's own documentation on audit, not least the *Notes for Guidance for Auditors*, is being wholly revised to accommodate differences in nomenclature and the greater diversity of the unified higher education sector. The content, style and coverage of audit reports have also been subject to review to ensure that they continue to offer clear, incisive and constructive comment. The first quality audits of the 'new' universities (scheduled for the Spring and Summer terms of 1993) will provide an early opportunity to assess the appropriateness of the audit methodology in these institutional contexts. The Division intends that information from these audits will be fed into a major review of the audit method to be undertaken in the summer of 1993, with a view to incorporating any necessary changes into the audit cycle from Autumn 1993 onwards.

This review will not be able to ignore other developments, which, by then, are likely to have established themselves as key features in the higher education landscape. One of the most important of these is the introduction of external quality assessment by the funding councils, as required by the 1992 Act, to provide a measure of discrimination on quality grounds in the allocation of teaching funds to higher education institutions. The juxtaposition of quality audit and assessment has sown seeds of confusion across the whole sector, and not only in those institutions brave and resilient enough to have played host to an audit team and an assessment panel within a short space of time. Quality assessment differs from audit both in its purpose and its focus.[9] It is intended as a means by which the quality of teaching and learning can be measured directly by subject peers acting on behalf of the funding council. Their task will be to inspect teaching and learning, programme by programme, and derive a single, composite measure (e.g. good, satisfactory, unsatisfactory), which will be taken into account when teaching funds are disbursed to institutions. At the time of writing, the detailed methodology to be employed by the funding councils for the purposes of quality assessment is not clear. The two rounds of pilot assessments revealed considerable potential overlap with quality audit as assessment panels sought to establish with reference to an institution's quality assurance mechanisms whether 'good' or 'bad' teaching was likely to be sustained, or improved, over time. The difference in the sense of ownership of the task (audit belongs with the institutions and is the responsibility of 'their' Council, responsibility for assessment lies with the funding bodies) may turn out to be crucial to its reception and impact on behaviour and attitudes towards improvement and enhancement. Logically the two processes are related, in the sense that any system for quality assurance may incorporate a means for assessing the quality of individual areas (be they subjects, programmes or research), including by making direct comparisons with appropriate and relevant activities elsewhere. The effectiveness of such comparisons and assessments as tools for quality assurance may well be an appropriate area for exploration during an external quality audit. Conversely, an external assessment team of the kind envisaged by the funding councils may find an external audit report of an institution's quality assurance systems an appropriate starting point for its inquiry into one or more areas within the institution. There may not be any inherent contradiction between the two processes. However, as both have come into operation at about the same time, and each is concerned to raise awareness and to stimulate further improvement by bringing external perspectives to bear on an institution's view of the quality of the teaching and learning that it provides, the scope for overlap, if not misunderstanding, appears quite considerable. The question that institutions will, no doubt, ask of each process is whether either, or both, will generate useful information and speed up its dissemination across the system to balance what might be seen as their intrusive effects and the additional costs incurred. For quality audit, the answer to such a question is (to borrow from the otherwise ill-fitting analogy with quality processes in the industrial sector) that quality is not without cost but that failure, or a decline in standards and the overall quality of the students' learning experience, would be far costlier. The experience of academic and quality audit so far has been one of having to rebut surprisingly few complaints about intrusiveness whilst receiving positive feedback from senior managers, staff and students that external audit has caused an institution to look at itself with a more critical eye. Unlike quality assessment, quality audit carries no direct penalty or reward. It has no means of forcing compliance with the findings of its teams, or even that audit reports be read and inwardly digested. Through the DQA, universities will be asked to provide a statement of action taken one year after the completion of an audit. Moreover, action taken and an institution's continuing reflection on its quality processes will form a major part of the agenda for the second audit. The experience of academic audit seems to show that the presentation of a well-founded and constructive analysis of a university's processes for quality assurance can act as an effective lever for change. We have seen the flurries caused by the establishment of audit and its advancement through the first cycle; it is, perhaps, in the second cycle where its capacity to serve as a real engine of change can be measured.

References

1. British Standards Institution (BSI) (1989) *Quality Systems Auditing*, British Standard 7229. London, BSI.
2. Entwhistle, N. (1992) *The Impact of Teaching on Learning Outcomes in Higher Education. A Literature Review*. Sheffield, CVCP University Staff Development Unit.
3. Williams, P. (1992) *CVCP Academic Audit Unit: Director's Annual Report*. Birmingham, CVCP Academic Audit Unit.
4. Jarratt, A. (1985) *Report of the Steering Committee for Efficiency Studies in Universities*. London, CVCP.
5. Reynolds, P.A. (Chairman) (1986) *Academic Standards in Universities*. London, CVCP.
6. Gregory, K. (1992) The initial reactions of a university to a pilot study by the CVCP Academic Audit Unit. In Banta, T. *et al. Proceedings of the Third International Conference on Assessing Quality in Higher Education*. Tennessee, Center for Assessment Research and Development.
7. Williams, P. (1992), see note 3.
8. Department of Education and Science (1991) *Higher Education: A New Framework*, White Paper Cmnd. 1541. London, HMSO.
9. HEFCE (1992) *Consultation Paper: Quality Assessment*. Bristol, HEFCE; SHEFC (1992) *Consultative Paper on Quality Assessment*. Edinburgh, SHEFC.

Part 3

Models from Beyond
British Higher Education

6

Quality and its Measurement:
A Business Perspective

Jim Finch

Introduction

The subject of quality is linked inextricably with the concept of measurement. However, many organizations seeking the quality accolade have watered down the notion of measurement in order to make it more palatable and more achievable. Quality organizations need to adopt a customer orientation. They will never achieve genuine quality if, in trying to measure the extent to which they satisfy their customers' needs, they use sloppy measurement techniques. Getting a reliable and useful measurement of such subjective views is difficult but essential. Techniques do exist and some of these are discussed in this chapter.

Quality framework

Any organization wishing to improve its level of Quality performance significantly, generally passes through five stages of development. While these are discussed as five distinct sections below, they are not a sequential set of separately performed discrete activities. The best analogue is that of a spiral of virtue. Each circuit of the spiral consists of all five activities in differing proportions, each traverse ending with the organization being in a better position to satisfy its customers and meet its competitors head-on.

Awareness

The first stage is awareness. This introduces members of the organization to the modern language, techniques and attitudes of Quality; in subsequent development of awareness, more advanced concepts of Quality are introduced as they become appropriate.

The business success of the Pacific Basin countries, which has been increasingly apparent since the late 1970s, has been closely linked to their obvious attention to a new concept of Quality. The definition of this new concept of Quality implied throughout this paper is best understood by dividing it into three distinct parts:

1. Understand what the customer values sufficiently to pay for in preference to all competitive offerings. Develop a precise specification for every aspect of this commodity.
2. Deliver this commodity exactly to specification 100 per cent of the time.
3. Improve the specification or reduce the cost to the customer faster than competition does.

Interpretation of this definition depends crucially on the scope of the commodity specification. If the attitude prevails that a product is a product is a product, then it is a specification for manufacturing. Total Quality management (TQM) is a term coined in the 1980s to counteract this restricted view of Quality. The specification must cover every aspect of an organization's activity, in terms of the customer's needs and wants. Assuming the student is the customer, the standards of buildings, meals, accommodation, career counselling, learning environment, staff attitudes and a myriad of other factors will be included in the specification for an educational organization, along with the more obvious ones of courses, lectures, research and qualifications. The weighting of the importance of these is determined by the customer.

The awareness stage is devoted mainly to training and must be led by executives, who will be responsible for developing the content of, and be first to participate in, the training programme. Topics for this training are:

1. Corporate Quality vision. The executives will share with the participants their vision of the Quality nirvana and convince the participants of their determination to change everything in the organization necessary to achieve it.
2. Executive and senior management leadership. This is the first and most important opportunity for management to signal their intention to bring about radical change in the culture of the organization, based on their concept of Quality.
3. Quality projects. Kaizen[1] is the Japanese name given to incremental improvement. Juran[2] states: 'Quality improvement can only be achieved project by project.' These are important notions to develop at the beginning of the journey to Quality. Two distinct types of project will be clearly differentiated:
   (a) Quality Improvement Project (QIP), which is selected by management and led by them;
   (b) Quality Circle (QC), which is selected by a natural work group to eliminate the myriad of problems they face within their daily work and constructively supported by management.

4. Initial Role of Measurement. This paper is directed at the role of measurement throughout the journey to Quality. In initial education there is a need to stress the role of measurement in the context of Quality Projects. Five important notions will be developed:

(a) 'If it cannot be measured, it cannot be controlled';

(b) there is a clear distinction between establishing and maintaining control. 'Out of control' is not used here in the modern business sense as a poor business position but in the statistical sense of the measurements falling outside the expected pattern with a frequency which exceeds that due to random variation;

(c) improvement of a process requires that the root causes of failures in the process are discovered and that the process is changed to eradicate these root causes. Western management has developed a penchant for applying solutions with insufficient evidence that the symptoms with which they are faced will be eliminated by the cure: falling student applications, increased school visits by teaching staff. What facts are known about the correlation between staff visits and student applications? Intuitively, most people would support the solution, but intuition proves to be a poor management tool;

(d) simple statistical techniques known for most of this century are still the most effective tools in the search for the root causes of Quality failure;

(e) once a measurement is 'in control', that is the variance has been reduced, it is almost certain that it will not be indicating that the results are as good as desired. In this case it is essential to find the process changes that will produce 'breakthrough'.[3]

Measurement methods

Immediately after awareness education, it is essential that the participants start to develop the skills of Quality projects. This quickly convinces the new Quality converts that the holy grail of root causes is difficult to attain. This naturally leads to a second wave of education and training in the tools of measurement based projects.

It is significant that both of the leading consultants who are acknowledged by the Japanese as the founding fathers of their Quality revolution are statisticians. Both preach the basic need for sound analytical techniques to be applied in order to find the elusive root causes.

These techniques have been known during most of this century and most were developed in Europe and America. The Japanese Union of Scientists and Engineers (JUSE) has formalized and popularized these techniques using the catchphrase 'The 7Q'[4] and incorporated them in a Quality project method.

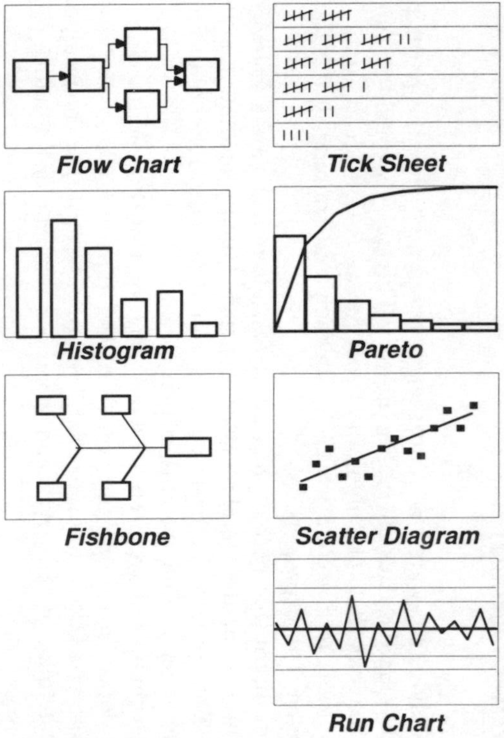

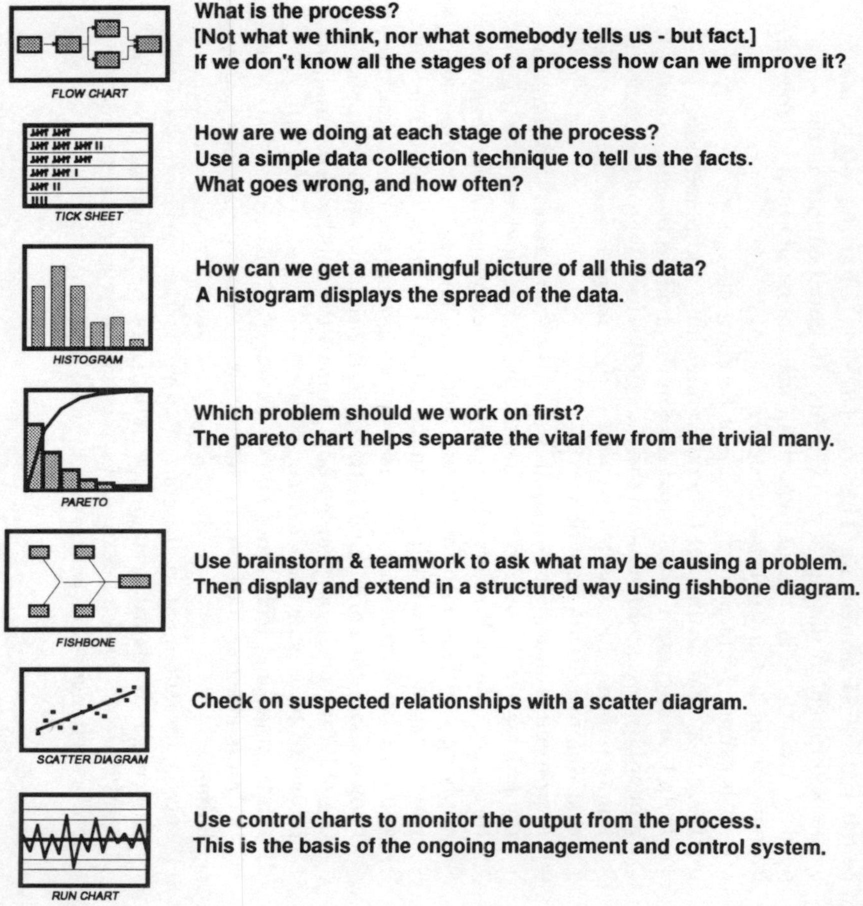

Flow Chart

Tick Sheet

Histogram

Pareto

Fishbone

Scatter Diagram

Run Chart

What is the process?
[Not what we think, nor what somebody tells us - but fact.]
If we don't know all the stages of a process how can we improve it?

How are we doing at each stage of the process?
Use a simple data collection technique to tell us the facts.
What goes wrong, and how often?

How can we get a meaningful picture of all this data?
A histogram displays the spread of the data.

Which problem should we work on first?
The pareto chart helps separate the vital few from the trivial many.

Use brainstorm & teamwork to ask what may be causing a problem.
Then display and extend in a structured way using fishbone diagram.

Check on suspected relationships with a scatter diagram.

Use control charts to monitor the output from the process.
This is the basis of the ongoing management and control system.

FLOW CHART

TICK SHEET

HISTOGRAM

PARETO

FISHBONE

SCATTER DIAGRAM

RUN CHART

Figure 6.1 (a) The 7Q; (b) why use the 7Q?

These comprise (Figure 6.1):

1. Process flowchart (the initial 7Q included graphs, but these were less well defined and, in the last few years, the process flowchart has been preferred).
2. Check sheet.
3. Histogram.
4. Pareto chart.
5. Ishikawa – cause and effect.
6. Scatter diagram.
7. Shewart control charts.

These relatively simple techniques appear to be readily understood when taught throughout an organization, but their subsequent application proves to be much more difficult to instil. Most of the effort in the measurement phase goes into changing the ingrained attitudes of business people, who are under pressure for short-term results to produce instant solutions to all problems. This has encouraged the development of action-based management and popular phrases such as 'paralysis by analysis' have contributed to the demotion of sound and rational business analysis. Action management is arguably the major 'root cause' of the inferior performance of Western business relative to that of the Pacific Rim countries.

Many analyses published in the 1980s showed that, in the average organization, which has carried out a Cost of Quality study, the combined cost of failure, appraisal and prevention is typically 20 per cent. It is reasonable to assume that this level of failure has continued for many years because, throughout the 1980s, the same level of failure has been consistently reported. During this period, many organizations attempted to improve their Quality, urged on by the popular press and various government initiatives.

Action management introduces permanent putative improvements to the way a company operates, so it would be reasonable to expect this failure to be a steadily reducing percentage of the organization's output, but this is manifestly not the case. Why? The reason can be found in Quality audits. Each innovation introduces its own constant level of failure. The process of innovation must be flawed and this indeed appears to be the case. The flaw is action management.

Thus, the objective in the measurement phase is to start to replace action management with factual management. Ishikawa acted as Quality consultant to the Japanese subsidiary of a major American manufacturing company for several years. For every proposal for improvement, presented to the local board, Ishikawa's contribution could be summed up in five words: 'What facts support this proposal?' In spite of the answer generally being inadequate, action management insisted on implementation. Eventually, Ishikawa regretfully withdrew his support.

Process focus

Two convergent developments are inexorably marching forward in the organization if the first two phases have been successful. These will require careful management to avoid conflict and disappointment when they meet.

The first development is in structured improvement work. A measure of the success of the awareness and measurement training is the speed at which Quality Improvement activity (whether Projects or Circles) spreads. In successful implementations, the problems being tackled cover a wide range of operational activities and there is a general air of progress.

The second development is in management involvement. The Quality revolution launched by the company's executives was triggered either by dissatisfaction with their own organization's performance or admiration of the performance of an organization they respect or fear; they have spent considerable time and effort on the initial training; they will have introduced Quality Councils at all levels in the company to support, encourage and co-ordinate these widespread activities.

A natural development is for the higher level Quality Councils to look for evidence that the pervasive measurement and project activity is improving the performance of the organization in the areas that were causing concern and led to the start of the Quality revolution. These areas represent implicit priorities that the executives have in mind, but which have not been expressed formally. The Quality Councils discover that the Quality activities are having a second-order beneficial effect on the factors the executives saw as important when they started the journey but do not seem to be addressing these areas directly. The executives were concerned that their share of government support was being reduced – the teaching departments have a thriving set of Quality projects to improve the way courses are developed.

It is important for senior management to be very sensitive at this stage as they manage the conflicting requirements of the new Quality practitioners' need to learn how to carry out successful QIPs and the executives' need to organize the projects to tackle the high priority items. Because the operational level projects have been chosen by local management, there is a great sense of ownership of the problem and this is an ideal condition within which to learn the Quality skills. The natural pace of Quality development helps to avoid this potential conflict because the two sets of participants require about the same length of time to carry out their own parallel developments. Setting the priorities for the organization is a task that is done in the boardroom or the Senate. The critical success factor (CSF)[5] technique is recommended to achieve this and is described below. The first CSF activity is for the executives to determine the set of processes by which they achieve their goals. Traditionally between 12 to 20 such processes are identified, and these must be managed by the executives themselves. A typical set of such processes for an education organization may be:

1. Manage strategic and period plan.
2. Manage general finance.
3. Allocate funds.
4. Initiate and design courses.
5. Develop programmes/courses.

6. Get programmes/courses approved.
7. Deliver programmes/courses.
8. Support courses.
9. Initiate and design research projects.
10. Get research approved.
11. Research.
12. Publish and commercialize research.
13. Recruit students.
14. Manage student welfare.
15. Recruit staff.
16. Develop staff capability.
17. Communicate internally and externally.
18. Maintain and develop real estate assets.
19. Maintain and develop information systems.

Be warned! Process analysis is a two-edged sword. It is a dangerous weapon if it becomes an exercise of analysis in its own right because excessive analysis leads to a minutiae that is not possible to manage. It is a powerful ally if it helps management to identify those activities that are crucial to the development of the organization and concentrate the limited improvement resources in those areas.

Four factors should guide the analysis of the processes:

1. Hierarchy. Each level of management should concentrate on its own level of the process structure. This is determined largely by the time required to make significant changes to performance. First-line management has a Quality improvement time horizon of weeks to months, middle management months to years, executive management years to decades.
2. Data and Product Flow. The process elements will have data and physical product flowing between them. It is beneficial to use the flows to develop the process map.
3. Process Limits. Each process activity will have a starting event and will be complete when it delivers an output to another part of the organization or to an outside customer. If it delivers to an internal customer then that customer has a dependency on that process to achieve its own objectives.

   This concept of dependency is one of the most important in the last two stages of Quality development, alignment of objectives and customer orientation, and will be developed further below. Successful understanding of dependency and responding to its requirements makes the difference between working for individual or functional excellence and working as a team. Are we recruiting top-performing students for the French course, the language department or the university?
4. Purpose. Ruthless honesty is the necessary ingredient for definition of purpose. It is not possible to improve a process where the purpose is not stated explicitly and where it does not reflect accurately the activities actually taking place. It will be impossible to improve a process of research project selection whose purpose is stated to be the development of

a new understanding of the flow of electrons in a superconductor if the real purpose is to gain the researchers more commercial sponsorship.

The major outcome of this process analysis is that the senior management will agree as a team:

1. Who is responsible for the major processes in the organization.
2. The location of significant interactions between the processes.
3. A firm set of priorities for improvements to the organization's performance.

The QIPs should be mapped against this process structure, and it will be obvious that there is a mismatch between the expectations of the executives and the activities of the QIP teams. When this mismatch is clearly understood, senior management can guide future projects into the priority areas. In the interim period, it is beneficial to allow the existing projects to come to their natural conclusion as the gain from the participants acquiring the skills of QIPs and the natural exhilaration from bringing their own projects to a successful conclusion far outweighs the short delay before they are deployed where the executives now know the action is needed.

Alignment of objectives

In outlining his controversial 14 points,[6] Deming denigrates the modern management idea prevalent in the West of Management By Objectives. Ishikawa[7] espoused a concept of management working as a close knit team, 'the woof and warp of the organisation', with a concerted strategy for an organization that every member understands and believes in completely. Ouchi[8] relates the results of one of his comparative studies showing a major difference between international American companies with Japanese subsidiaries and international Japanese companies with American subsidiaries. The difference is that the American owners do not believe their Japanese subsidiaries understand the concept of strategy, and the Japanese owners have the same doubts about the American subsidiaries. Ouchi concludes that in American companies, the strategy is written down and reviewed by management as part of a formal strategic planning activity. It is then changed or ignored to meet the exigencies of short term pressures. The Japanese company does not rely on written strategy but expects it to be lived and breathed by every member of the organization for decades or centuries. When the chief executive of a major Japanese corporation responded to the question 'What is the strategy of your company?' his revealing reply was 'To be in business 1000 years from now.'

These examples show the concern of Quality experts with the conflict between the desire for a team approach for the good of the organization and the fact that, in the West, Taylorism has conditioned us to partition work by function and to strive for short-time functional excellence.

The process work described above will bring these ideas into sharp focus. Whichever way the processes are analysed, it will not be possible to arrange the processes to fit any management structure. Processes are inevitably cross-functional activities. Support processes, e.g. 'manage the organization's finance', will inevitably interact with all other processes. If the process to deliver education courses attempts to embrace its own finance management, there will not be an adequate mechanism to ensure the finances are optimized throughout the organization. In spite of this, so strong is the Taylorist instinct that most managers initially embrace process management by trying to force-fit the process structure and the hierarchical management structure. This appears to be an effort to maintain their tribal boundaries.

Functional excellence is a very poor suboptimization of an organization. The sales director is aware of the importance of the new product being introduced to the future well-being of the organization. She/he determines to make it the most impressive product launch in the company's history. The research and development director knows this is a major technology leap for the company and prepares to follow up the launch with the key customers, as this is the most his/her resources can support. The finance director is keenly aware that the company has stretched itself to develop this product and intends to set very stringent budgets as the product is launched and release funds to market development in a tightly controlled manner. The personnel director is aware that the workforce is going to find the new technology very demanding and is determined to ensure every member of the company will undergo fundamental retraining to meet the challenge or morale will drop steeply.

Traditionally each of these directors then sets out independently to achieve his/her worthy goal, but this is a recipe for disaster. It even has a popular sobriquet – check and balance. The hapless planner has tried all the accepted budget and plan techniques to mitigate this looming conflict but conflict management is still the final prevailing technique.

One thing is certain: in this fierce conflict, one sure loser is Quality. Hotels will be booked for the launch but the finance director will prevail and some will be cancelled. The development support department is overstretched because the launch is very successful in sales terms but the number of customers to support far exceeds the development plan. Finance recognize a success in sales but have to stretch their financial position beyond what the director judges is prudent. Of course the direct support staff cancel their courses.

Let us consider how the CSF method can orchestrate a team approach to organization management. Figure 6.2 shows a matrix of the processes by which the organization operates, against the key factors that are critical to the success of the organization. The processes derive from the work outlined above. The Critical Success Factors are derived, along with a formal statement of the mission of the organization, in workshops for the top management team. Both of these activities require considerable effort, technique and care, the details of which are not appropriate here.

Once the matrix is established and agreed by the management team, it is possible, by techniques based on Delphi methods, to determine the key nodes

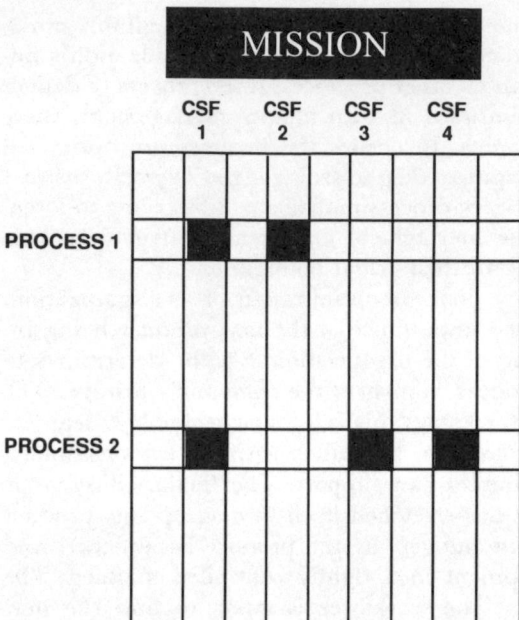

Figure 6.2 CSF – Mission – Process.

of the matrix. These are indicated by the solid squares. The key nodes in a row show where the management team believes the top priority areas for improvement of each process lie. The key nodes in a column show which process areas have the maximum impact on the CSFs. It is the interaction of these nodes that makes or breaks a team approach.

Because processes are unconditionally cross-functional, the key nodes in a row will be managed by different functions. The team cannot function if the dependencies between the key nodes within a row are not understood and do not form part of a cross-functional service level agreement.

Key nodes in a column likewise show the cross-process dependency. When top management apply the time and effort to develop, understand and believe in their mutual dependency illustrated by this technique, Taylorism will have run its course and a more productive team approach to business will develop in the organization.

Using the matrix, it is possible to address one of Deming's 14 points. The synergistic objectives of management can be set from the matrix providing the predominant emphasis is on achieving that part of a manager's objectives on which the customer (or another manager) depends. Aligned objectives require the objectives to be achieved and the dependencies to be fulfilled in a carefully balanced manner.

Customer orientation

Surprisingly, the customer is the area where many organizations elect to start their Quality activity. This is equivalent to giving first year medical students their first practical surgical experience by asking them to remove a tumour from the brain of a living patient.

It is too easy to identify a set of customers and ask them a plethora of questions related to that organization's services, people, products and attitudes. Any market research company is more than willing to undertake the survey and 'analyse' the results. The difficulty with this approach is two-fold. First the customers express their opinions in their own terms and it is extremely difficult to translate these into recognizable actions the company can take. For example, a customer wants a 'smooth ride'. Does this mean crankshafts have to be ground to a millionth of an inch, the upholstery has to be made thicker or the suspension made more compliant? In fact, in this case, the customers did not like the way the brakes were too fierce on the present model. The organization could have spent a fortune on upholstery, engine and suspension when they needed to work on the brakes! A technique for handling this problem – Quality Function Deployment[9] – has been developed by Toyota. It is being steadily bastardized in the West and is degenerating into a development and marketing activity, whereas it is essential it is a company-wide activity.

Second, the questions are invariably expressed in organization structure terms: 'How do you believe our receptionists greeted you on arrival?' Should the receptionist have been the initial contact?

A lot of experience is essential in the basic techniques of Root Cause Analysis in order to tackle relatively minor issues like 'the complete failure of last year's business plan' before raising expectations in the customer which the burgeoning Quality skills of the organization are not yet ready to meet. Application of measurement and Quality techniques in this most difficult area of an organization is not discussed any further here.

The place of measurement

Measurement is pervasive in any successful drive for Quality. Its use can now be discussed against the framework discussed on page 63.

Within a Quality project

A project should have a set of well defined activities and a discipline must be in place to ensure that sound numeric evidence of successful completion of each phase is available before the project moves to the next. An excellent basis for the project structure is based on the 7Q discussed on page 65.

This schematic of the essential steps of a project shows the importance of measurements (Figure 6.3). Generalizing the concept above that the customer

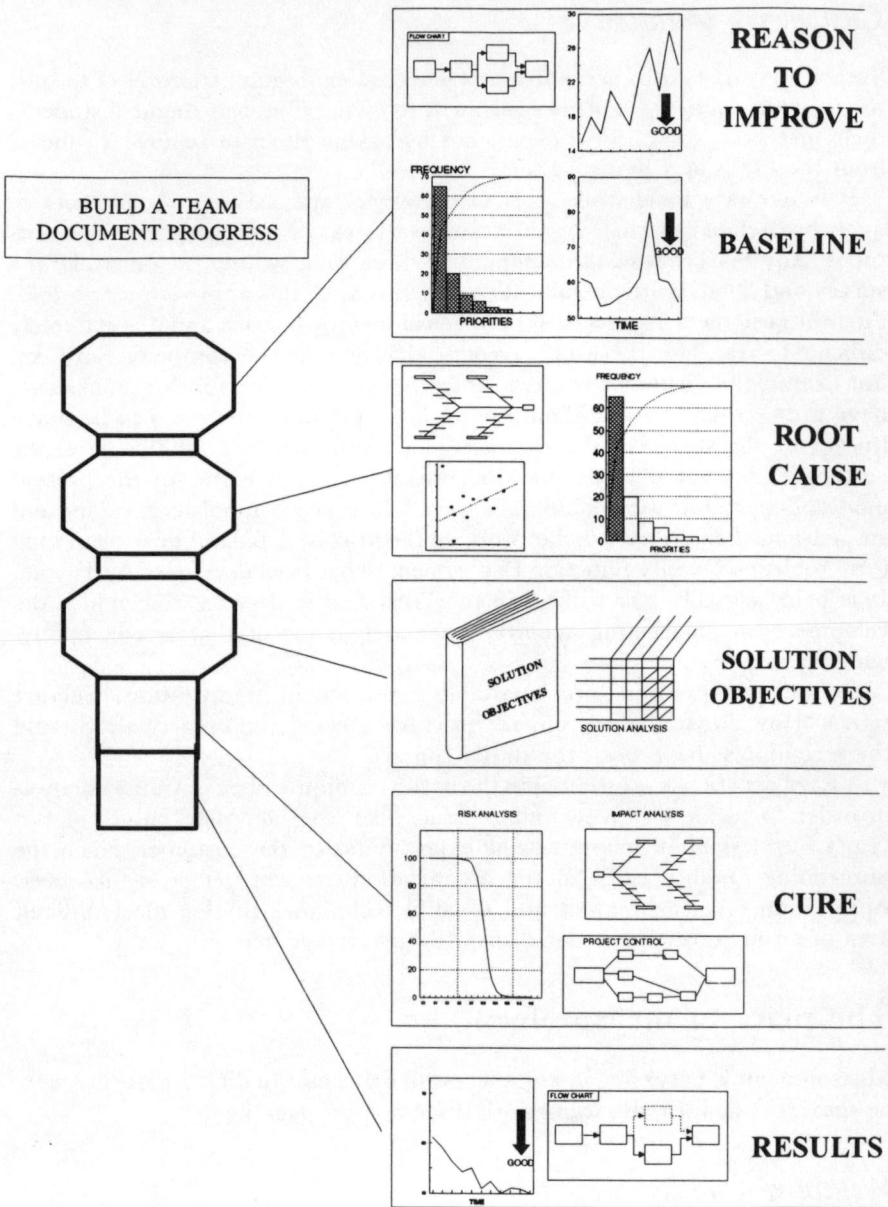

Figure 6.3   Quality project method.

is unable to express his wants in terms that the organization can immediately interpret, so it is with all incipient Quality problems. They are invariably first stated as a general disquiet with the status quo. For example 'students with high incoming qualifications on a degree course are exhibiting a high drop-out rate'. Such is the nature of human intuitive judgement that it is highly likely that this conclusion is not supported by the facts. A small number of such students have all left recently and the conclusion is drawn.

Phase I – proof of need

The first phase is to convert these general feelings of unease into firm in-controvertible fact. The rule of thumb associated with the statistics of control charts is that there must be about 20 measurements[10] to have a chance of seeing sporadic failure or trends outside the random variability of the process. Here we come up against one of the most difficult factors of this measurement-based regime. In degree courses we probably only record achievements yearly, or even three-yearly. Do we have to wait 60 years to establish confidence that we have a trend in our degree drop-out performance? The immediate answer is 'Yes, if it is not possible to change the measuring system.' To executives in the organization this is unacceptable, and they resort to 'business judgement' or, to use a less flattering but more accurate description, 'a guess'. This is nearly always to do something, and I suggest it is the root cause of the poor, action-oriented management performance in the discussion above.

Obviously, the measurement process can be changed by widening the sample to include ten other, similar, departments or universities and using simple tests of significance or analysis of variance to prove or disprove the hypothesis, but this means a determined effort to institute a new measurement system. It is also possible that historic records can increase the sample to a statistically significant degree.

A final and popular alternative is to conclude that this project is too intransigent because it cannot be measured, so another project is chosen. In the first few years of Quality development this is a very acceptable solution, because so many things are identified as high priority that it is advantageous to start by gathering the low-hanging fruit. If the measurement is particularly difficult, then it is likely that the alternative project will yield a better return on the effort invested.

Once a suitable measurement is established, which provides conclusive evidence of the need to improve, then the process that delivers the result being measured should be analysed and documented.

Process analysis invariably shows that the effect is not correlated directly with a single activity in the process, and it is possible to produce a Pareto chart of the number of process failures as against the type of failure. Possible reasons given in records of why students drop out may include accommodation, involvement with drugs, clash with lecturers, health, financial difficulties and others. The Pareto chart is used to find the essential few to prioritize the work.

It only remains to measure the trend in the chosen parameter, say financial difficulties, and Phase I is complete. Projects should be signed off by a review manager at each stage; not as a check on progress but to provide help and encouragement to the project team if the project is proving difficult, as many do. The most obvious sign of difficulty is when the team attempt to close off a phase without sound measurements leading to their conclusions.

Phase II – root cause

Ishikawa gave his name to the most powerful method known for helping to organize the thought processes required to postulate potential root causes (the fishbone or cause and effect diagram). This is an intuitive analysis and is not strictly a measurement technique but it is regarded as an essential tool in the toolbag of Quality project teams.

When the areas to concentrate on are selected from the fishbone diagram, (see Figure 6.1), then measurements are essential to corroborate the hypo-thesis of the cause of the problem to the known facts. The correlation diagram is the preferred tool and is the required minimum. If the project team is statistically sophisticated then many other analytical techniques can augment the analysis.

The Pareto chart is used to determine the priority for improvement by relating the number of times the various areas of the fishbone contribute to the problem area defined in the objective box on the extreme right of the diagram. This second phase is generally the longest in a Quality project and typically takes about 50 per cent of the total project time.

Phase III – solution objectives

No formal measurements are expected for this phase but the objectives must be stated in measurable terms, which will establish the limits of the cost and benefits of the cure. The most important feature of the solution objectives is the differentiation between *musts* and *wants*, which help to choose the most cost-effective, least-risk cure.

Phase IV – the cure

There are many potential cures available for any root cause (including the intuitive one we first thought of). Each cure must satisfy all the musts dis-cussed above; each will satisfy more or less of the wants.

No cure will be risk-free and as risk-averse managers we will favour the one that minimizes our risk – but how often is a risk analysis carried out before a business decision is made? A few perfunctory what-if questions may be answered by using a spreadsheet but the choice of a cure is generally part of the initial 'guess'.

Any cure will have both positive and negative impacts on the organization and its subpopulations. The reverse Ishikawa diagram is very powerful for assessing the ratio of the good and bad effects.

Finally, the cure will not be effected instantaneously with the expenditure of zero resources: project control methods are necessary to manage the time and resources. It is instructive to observe many Quality projects where, at the outset, the team has drawn a Pert or precedence control chart for a project where the unknowns outweigh the known factors by many orders of magnitude. Formal project control is only relevant where the problem and objectives are well understood.

Phase V – results

The project is not complete until the control measurement clearly show the results proposed in the solution objectives document are being achieved.

All improvements in Quality are due to improvements in the process that delivers the results. It is essential that the new process is different from the original one and the changes must be visible and documented. This is a sure test of the reality of the cure. Many so-called Quality solutions are the application of extra management attention. This is never a cure; when the attention is diverted to the next crisis the process reverts to its previous unacceptable state. Attention by managers or non-managers is never a solution to Quality. This was the Achilles heel of the 1950s reliance on Quality inspection; people paid to apply attention only have a very limited ability to identify Quality failures.

Process progress

When a sufficiently large number of projects are measurably improving individual parts of a process, it is only reasonable to expect that, at the macro level, the overall process should show improvements.

Three measurements should be sufficient to characterize the performance of the process:

1. How much of the purpose is being achieved with how much resource: the efficiency.
2. How much of the purpose is being achieved acceptable to the customer and how much is subject to scrap and rework: the effectiveness.
3. How long does the process take and how much of that time is the processed product in a wait state: process time versus entitlement.

As organization processes are owned by executives, this ownership should be made glaringly visible throughout the organization and to the customers

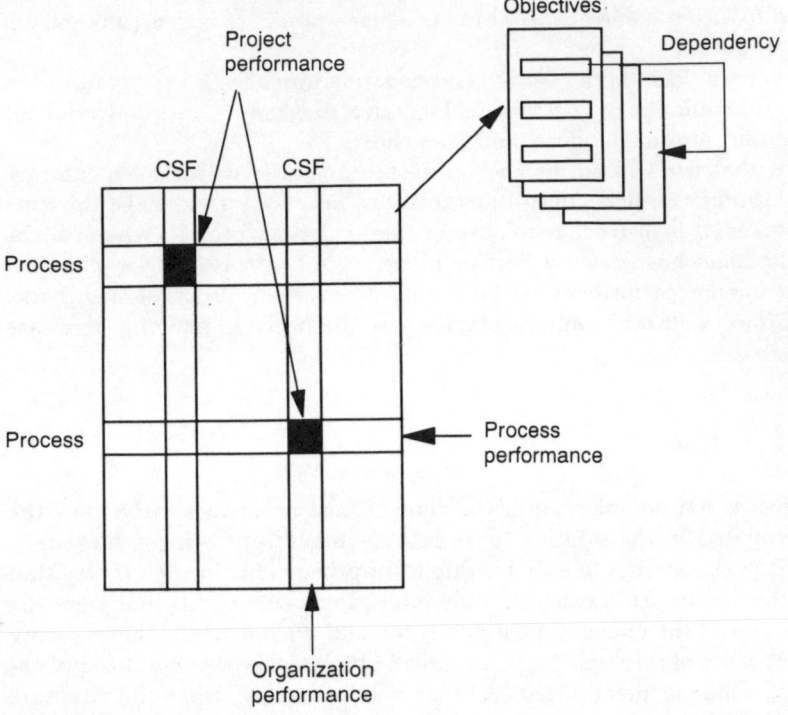

Figure 6.4   Objectives from CSFs.

outside when the time is ripe. Process owners should display the three process performance measures they choose in a very prominent position throughout the organization. This public declaration is a powerful rallying flag for people involved in the process, the customers of the process and the other process owners who are dependent on the performance of that process for the well-being of their own process.

Critical success factors

The mission and the critical success factors are agreed by the most senior management group in the organization. Measurements of these will be of a long-term nature as they represent the strategic endeavour of the organization.

The clearest way to understand these ultimate objectives is that they are the ones the board is supporting the chief executive to achieve. Typically these relate to the fabric of the organization in terms of capital and people assets, the attitude to customers is generally included and some key performance criteria, such as growth, competitive performance, profit.

The relationship between these objectives and the CSFs is very close and it is often expedient to couch the measurements of the objectives in terms of the degree of goodness of the CSFs (Figure 6.4).

Again these CSFs must be understood by all members of the organization and the performance against the Chief Executive's measurement criteria must be visible to all. An ideal place to display these objectives and measurements is in the canteen, the entrance hall of major buildings and in the company or organization's published performance results.

Customer effect

As stated on page 73, it is very odd how an organization new to Quality feels it can involve its customers when they are the ones who are most painfully aware of its failures. Certainly all measurements must be moved from the classic internal measurements 'How many did we make against plan?' to the customer-oriented measurements 'What percentage of what we made did not meet all the customers' requirements?'

Customer surveys are inherently dangerous measurements as they establish unfulfillable expectations and, because of the imprecision of the questions and replies, it is extremely difficult to interpret the customers' intended responses. The problem is further compounded because the performance of the commodity in the marketplace is not statistically correlated with the findings of such surveys. Only when the organization has achieved an adequate level of Quality capability is it time to involve the customers, using a comprehensive set of techniques throughout the whole organization based on the Quality Function Deployment model.

Measurement summary

Figure 6.4 shows the interaction of the measurements discussed:

1. Projects improve the priority areas of the business indicated by those nodes where the performance of a process is critical to the achievement of the CSF.
2. The sum of the projects within a process improves the process performance. The process owner is required to support these projects and ensure they are directed to the highest priority areas.
3. The sum of the process owner activities in a vertical column is the joint responsibility of the executive team to ensure the strategic objectives of the organisation are achieved.

References

1. Masaaki, I. (1986) *Kaizen*. London, Random House.
2. Juran, J.M. (1964) *Managerial Breakthrough*. New Delhi, McGraw-Hill Book Co.
3. Juran, J.M. and Gryna, F.M. Jr (1982) *Quality Planning and Analysis*, 2nd edn. Tata McGraw-Hill Publishing Co. Ltd.

4. Burr, J.T. *et al.* (1990) The tools of quality. *Quality Progress.*
5. Hardaker, M. and Ward, J.M. (1989) Building a team. *Harvard Business Review.*
6. Deming, W.E. (1986) *Out of the Crisis.* Cambridge, MA, MIT Centre for Advanced Engineering Study.
7. Ishikawa, K. (1985) *What is Total Quality Control?* (Trans. D. J. Lu). Prentice Hall.
8. Ouchi, W. (1986) *London Lecture Tour.*
9. Sullivan, L.P. (1986) Quality function deployment. *Quality Progress.*
10. Shewart, W.A. (1931) *The Economics of Control of Quality of Manufactured Products.* New York, D. Van Nostrand Co. Inc.

7

Royal Mail: Developing a Total Quality Organization

Ian Raisbeck

The purpose of this chapter is to share with you the changes taking place at the Royal Mail as it pursues its basic business strategy of being a total quality organization.

The business

To emphasize the significance of the changes that such a commitment entails, it might be helpful if I provided a few key facts about Royal Mail:

1. It is the largest component business of the Post Office.
2. Its origins can be traced back 350 years.
3. It employs 170,000 people.
4. It is profitable.
5. It delivers 64 million items per day, with 100,000 collection points and 24 million delivery points.
6. Its monopoly powers provide significant protection.

The other component businesses of the Post Office are Parcelforce and Post Office Counters Limited. It is worth noting that the Post Office has been profitable for a considerable number of years, and that this is somewhat unusual amongst postal administrations.

In late 1987 and 1988 Royal Mail recognized the need for change. It was continuing to grow but only because the market was growing faster than its own share was declining. Of particular significance was the very explicit customer dissatisfaction, often shown through direct complaint and substantial numbers of column inches of negative comment in the national and local press. Employee dissatisfaction was also clearly demonstrated, through high turnover and large numbers of industrial disputes, with a national strike in August 1988. The combination of customer dissatisfaction and industrial action was causing the monopoly to come under threat.

Developing a Total Quality direction

A number of foundations were established for the development of the Total Quality direction for Royal Mail.

First, clear definitions of the current state of the business and the future desired state (the vision) were created. These were created using small groups of senior and middle managers and other employees working together over a day-and-a-half period. This was important to establish the strengths of the Royal Mail that had to be maintained in any future direction, as well as identifying those areas that needed to be improved.

The second element was the creation of the mission and values for Royal Mail. At that time no mission or values existed and, in fact, nowhere did we have clear statements in respect of the value we placed on our customers or our employees. This area will be discussed later. The third element comprised certain agreed definitions of what total quality means. These are in the form of statements that can be discussed and bring out the key elements of any total quality approach. Fourth, and of extreme importance, was to gain the agreement that there is interdependence between achieving and maintaining long-term customer satisfaction and the establishment and maintenance of employee satisfaction. Fifth, certain proven processes, tools and techniques common to many other total quality approaches in successful organizations, were to be included.

This whole approach was then put together with substantial involvement from senior directors. Each assigned one of their direct reports for approximately three months to a team that put together the direction. They worked within the team on Tuesday, Wednesday and Thursday, spending the other days of the week back with their colleagues testing out the thoughts and approaches that were being proposed.

At Royal Mail, we define total quality as a way of working that enables the organization to achieve its mission in a manner consistent with its values. Implicit with mission are the objectives, targets and goals that relate to the key elements of the mission statement itself. The Royal Mail mission and values relate to its four stakeholders:

1. Customer.
2. Employee.
3. Shareholder.
4. Community.

These stakeholders are the same for most, if not all, businesses and organizations. The difference between organizations is one of emphasis. For example, in the case of the Royal Mail we have a single shareholder, namely the government. Because of the positioning of our organization, we possibly need to place greater emphasis on the community as a stakeholder than would be the case for some commercial organizations.

The Royal Mail mission and values

Our mission is one of being recognized as the best organization in the world in our area of activity. Probably more important in practical terms are the enabling elements by which this mission will be achieved. These cover the need to excel in our basic processes, the need to form partnerships with customers, the requirement to be a profitable organization for long-term viability and reinvestment, the creation of a positive working environment for all employees linked to the satisfaction of our customers, the role within the community and finally the need to be both forward looking and innovative. The Royal Mail business values are:

1. Our customers and their requirements for:
   (a) reliability;
   (b) value for money;
   (c) accessibility;
   (d) courtesy;
   (e) integrity;
   (f) security;
   (g) prompt and timely response.
2. All our fellow employees and their needs for:
   (a) respect;
   (b) training and development;
   (c) involvement;
   (d) recognition and reward.
3. The way we do our job and the way it affects our customers both inside and outside the business.

These business values relate particularly to our concern and care for our customers and their requirements and also for all our fellow employees. Emphasis is placed on the fact that we are all employees and that there is not a split between managers and operational employees. These elements are of particular importance in terms of creating the employee environment.

It is worth noting that while the mission and values were created in the middle of 1988, they were not broadly displayed within the Royal Mail until 1990. This was a conscious decision, because it was felt that there had to be some clearly demonstrated moves, particularly in respect of the employee values, if there was not to be a cynical reaction to their display.

Defining total quality

At Royal Mail, we define total quality as:

1. A comprehensive way of working throughout the organization, which allows all employees as individuals and as teams to add value and satisfy the needs of their customers.

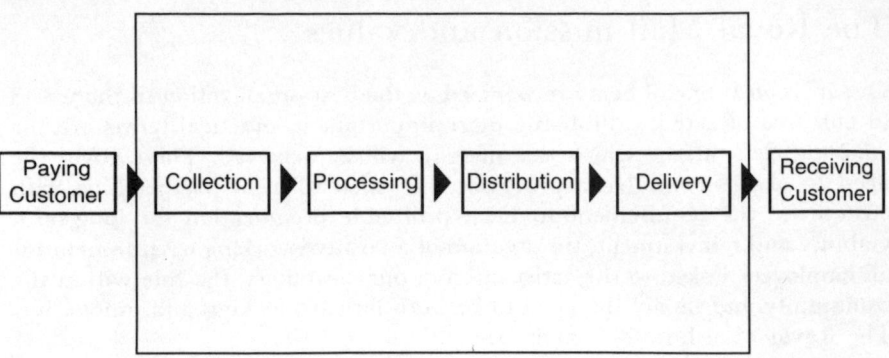

Figure 7.1   Basic operational process.

2. A business-wide customer-driven strategy of change, which moves us progressively to an environment where a steady and continuous improvement
   of everything we do is a way of life.
3. Identifying and satisfying the needs of the customer starting with the
   external customer and working backwards so that quality at each step is
   defined in terms of the 'next customer' in the process.
4. Being both effective (delivering the right products to the right segments of
   the market) and efficient (doing so at the most economical levels possible).

These statements place emphasis on the fact that total quality represents a
strategy of change that is customer-based. It places great emphasis on employees as individuals and as teams being concerned about adding value and
satisfying the needs of their customers. The statements also clearly describe
the internal customer concept, starting from the external customer and then
working backwards through the organization. The final statement defines the
need not only to be effective but efficient. We are talking of total quality as
a long-term way of working that enables the organization to be successful.
There is often a danger in total quality that too much emphasis is placed on
being effective and the internal values, sometimes called the softer elements,
and insufficient emphasis placed on the need to be efficient. Emphasis on the
latter results in the elimination of low- and zero-added-value activities within
the organization. Efficiency and effectiveness are key and complementary
requirements.

   Figure 7.1 shows the basic operational process and demonstrates that it
is a very clearly defined set of supplier–customer relationships. The key element is that as an organization we have two customers – the paying customer
and the receiving customer. Our delivery postmen clearly perceive the receiving customer as their primary customer. For example, they sometimes cannot
perceive that it is a basic requirement of the receiving customer to receive a
bill on a Saturday morning. This is true unless they appreciate the requirements of the paying customer in terms of the timing of receipt of the item they

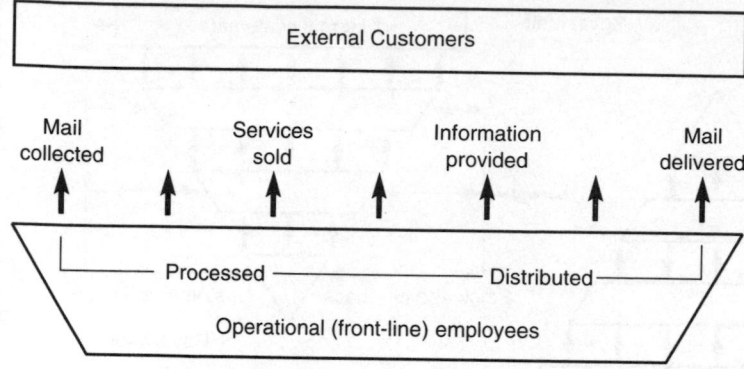

Figure 7.2 Customer interface.

are issuing, and the subsequent implications in terms of payment timing, cash flow and so on.

Figure 7.2 shows the basic interface that determines the success of the organization. It is these millions of individual interactions each day, covering mail collection and delivery, the sale of our services, the provision of information and dealing with customer problems, that determine whether our organization is perceived as providing an overall effective service. This interface between ourselves and our external customers is the fundamental interface of the organization and we have some 140,000 employees operating at this interface level, including those who work in processing units. In addition, 30,000 work in management and support functions. Those management and support functions exist to support the effectiveness of the interface with the external customer. It is critical for management teams and support functions to clearly define their outputs, in other words, what it is they do, in the context of providing support for front-line employees. Traditionally, senior management teams have often thought of themselves as providing the products and services direct to external customers, rather than the actions that they need to take to enable others to provide those services. The major functions also need to think in terms of their outputs, so that those outputs focus towards the external customer and provide the internal customers with the support required to meet the needs of those external customers.

Figure 7.3 shows the two extremes of organizational culture. The left-hand diagram shows the organization pressing down on the external customer. While the activities at the interface remain as described in Figure 7.2, it indicates that many junior and middle managers felt that they worked for their boss. Consequently, the arrows indicate workflows up through the organization. As one individual noted when first seeing this diagram, in a monopoly organization 'the top team could be dead for two years and one would not notice'. This is also probably true for many large organizations in the non-public sector.

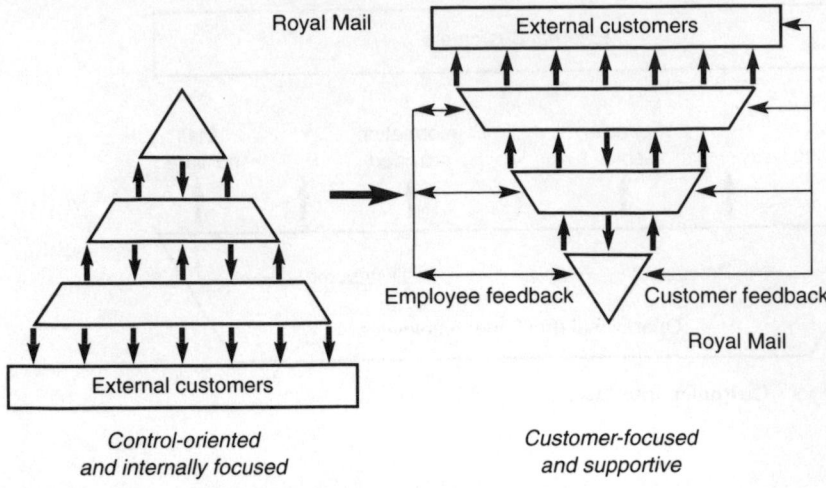

Figure 7.3 Required organizational change.

The right-hand diagram shows the external customers as the focus of the organization, with the organization utilizing customer and employee feedback systems as key elements in decision-making. The predominant focus of senior and middle management, together with the support functions, is focused towards the external customer interface.

Putting the customer first

On 26 September 1988, the Senior Management of Royal Mail took the following decision:

> The Letters Management Committee agrees that 'Customer First', the Total Quality Process for Royal Mail describes the way of working that will enable the business to achieve its mission and objectives. The members commit on a team and individual basis to positively pursue all the actions necessary to fully implement the process.

The 'cause and effect' diagram (Figure 7.4) shows all those areas that must be addressed in an integrated manner if the Royal Mail is to make effective progress towards becoming a total quality organization. The agreed strategy document takes each of these areas and describes the key directions that the business requires to follow in order to become a total quality organization. Each of these areas is discussed in more detail later.

Measurement

One key element that runs throughout the Royal Mail approach to total quality is that of measurement. This is essential to allow judgements to be

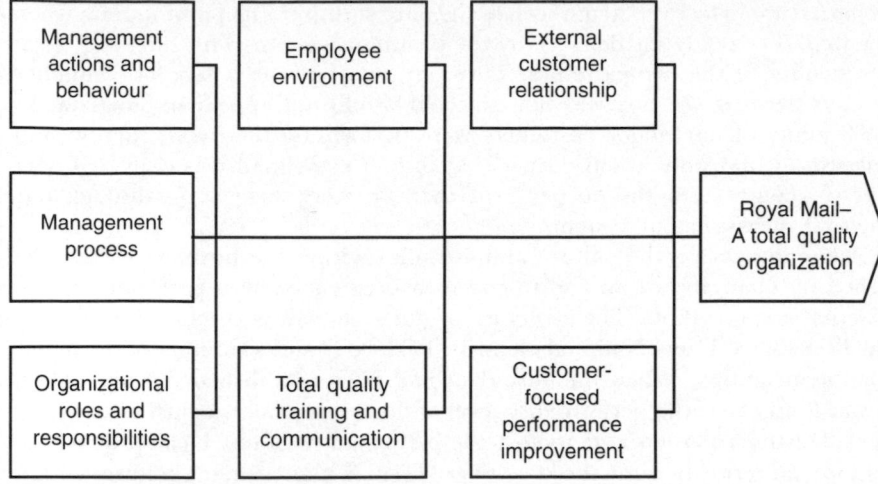

Figure 7.4 The cause and effect diagram.

made in order to act to change things. Throughout the rest of this chapter, particularly in relation to the customer, the employee and management actions and behaviour, examples are provided of measurements introduced to date in Royal Mail.

External customer relationship

A Customer First direction was established for each of the five key elements of the external customer relationship, that is:

1. Identification of requirements.
2. Product development.
3. Measurement of customer satisfaction.
4. Communications.
5. Image.

If we take as an example measurement of customer satisfaction, the Customer First direction established in the strategy document stated:

> The business will progressively develop and maintain an objective structured measure of customer satisfaction covering all aspects of our performance interface with the external customer for interpretation, analysis and feedback to management for action.

Let us now focus on some of the measurements that have been introduced at this key interface. Up to 1988 the Royal Mail measured the performance of its basic products (first and second class mail) by the time taken from the point in time when the item receives the date stamp to the point in time when the item was ready for delivery by the postman/woman. This obviously took no account of the two extremes. Thus, an item lying in a box for a number of days because the box was not collected would not appear in our data. In 1988 many of our major customers were performing their own surveys and suggesting that only about 70 per cent of first class mail was delivered next day, in contrast to the 90 per cent that we were suggesting through our internal measurement system.

A key impact on the culture and attitudes within the business was established by changing to an end-to-end measurement system performed by an external organization. The structure of the system was discussed with both the Post Office Users National Council (POUNC) and a number of the major mail associations. When the base data had been established during 1988–9 it was found that the performance level of first class mail was just over 74 per cent. During 1989–90 and 1990–1 the performance of our basic products in end-to-end terms became the key driver of senior management bonuses within the Royal Mail, and also the primary focus of improvement activities. Prior to that time the primary driver of bonus for managers had related to the achievement of cost budget.

When performance was measured at the end of the financial year 1991–2, it was clear that the first class letter mail reliability had been improved almost 16 points during that three-year period. Comparative performance measures across Europe showed that the Royal Mail letter reliability compared very favourably with those of other major European Postal Administrations (Figure 7.5). Results at the end of financial year 1992–3 show that the improving trend has continued with almost 92 per cent of first class items delivered next day.

Customer satisfaction

As indicated previously, the Royal Mail set itself a basic direction of introducing a structured measure of customer satisfaction which covers all aspects of our performance and interface with the external customer. The customer perception index represents such an instrument. This index has been introduced progressively through the Royal Mail and, from the beginning of the 1991 calendar year, has been in operation throughout the Royal Mail. Figures 7.6 and 7.7 show the responses in a particular quarter for the social customers and business customers in the Brighton postcode area. Based on research for each class of customer, 1000 value points were spread amongst the key factors that influence our relationship with our customers. The results of questionnaires sent to our social customers and business customers in each postcode area are converted into a score out of 100 for each of those key elements. The diagrams show the results for one area for the first eight most important elements for social customers and the first ten most important elements for business customers. This data is used as a primary driver of improvement activities in a local postcode area situation.

Overall % delivered next working day

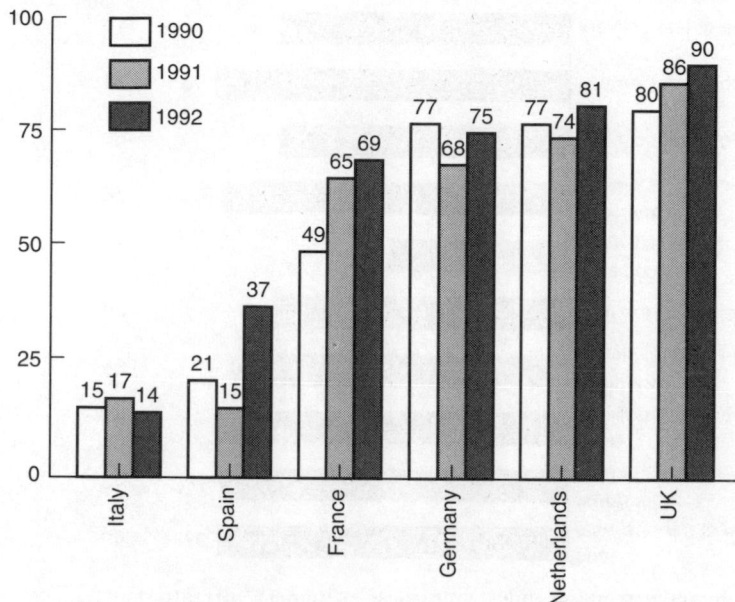

Figure 7.5 European end-to-end quality of service 1992

Social customers (Brighton)

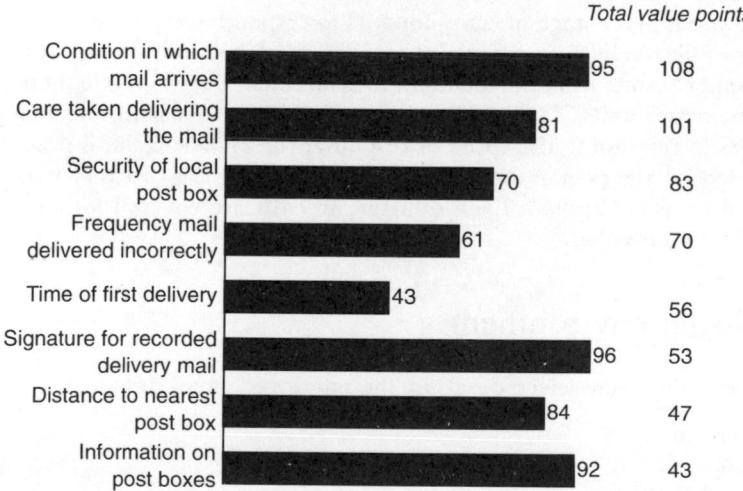

Figure 7.6 Customer perception index – social customers (Brighton).

Figure 7.7   Customer perception index – business customers (Brighton).

Two other measurements that operate in relation to the interface with the external customer are the customer satisfaction index and the mystery telephone shopper. First, the customer satisfaction index indicates how effective we are in dealing with customer complaints. This information is obtained by asking a substantial percentage of complainants to respond and give us information on how effectively their complaint was handled. Second, the mystery telephone shopper results from independent measurement based on telephone calls to customer care units. The individual making the call measures against key parameters in relation to the speed of response, the knowledge and information provided by the person answering at the unit and the courtesy with which the enquiry was handled. Each quarter, 40 calls are covered for each unit and feedback provided.

The employee environment

Nine key areas have been selected within the employee environment:

1. Pay and reward.
2. Recognition.
3. Training and development.
4. Involvement.

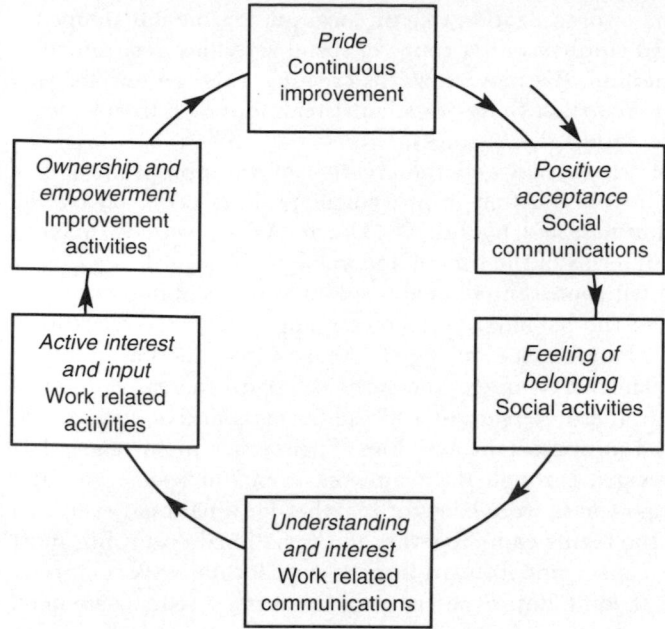

Figure 7.8 Involvement.

5. Organizational relationships.
6. Workplace environment.
7. Health, welfare and safety.
8. Involvement in the community.
9. Internal communications.

Again, for each of these areas, a Customer First direction was established in the strategy document. For example, if we look at recognition, the basic direction stated 'through the provision of a recognition framework and the training of all managers the business will become a recognition focused organization'. Each one of the nine elements could be the subject of substantial discussion in its own right. Let us consider just one area, that of involvement.

The main elements in the creation of an environment for involvement are illustrated in Figure 7.8. It is important to recall that the initial strategic direction was established in September 1988, just after a national strike of our operational employees. To create an atmosphere for involvement within Royal Mail it has been necessary to adopt a step-by-step approach. As far as operational employees are concerned we have placed particular emphasis on initially gaining an improved social relationship and a feeling of social belonging. This has included the improvement of many of the basic elements in areas such as the provision of improved uniforms, shoes and trainers. We have also created a leisure magazine, which incorporates the use of our buying power as a major organization to gain local purchasing advantage for employees, and placed emphasis on a range of social activities determined at the local level. In addition, the move towards creating a recognition-focused environment has included such things as a consistent approach to our recognition of long service within the business.

The whole area of recognition and the creation of an appropriate policy and framework was one of the first improvement projects taken on by the senior team of the business led by Bill Cockburn. As a result, we have a consistent approach in terms of the timing and value of the awards associated with long service but with substantial local freedom in terms of how these are introduced. Because of the backlog, over 60,000 employees were recognized for various periods of long service during the year of introduction in 1990.

As social interest and involvement increases so, then, increased interest develops in relation to the understanding of the business and active participation in work-related improvement activities. Such active involvement has been clearly demonstrated through the teamwork events of 1990, 1991 and 1992. In 1990, some 50 teams were brought together for a national event. In 1991 and 1992 over 100 teams came together in the national event, but most important those 100 teams came forward from over 50 local events. The 1992 event showed the first joint improvement projects formed with customers, and over two days was visited by 10,000 employees and customers. So, as we move round the circle, and every element in this circle of involvement is kept going, we progressively move to an increasing number of employees (managerial and operational) feeling a greater ownership and empowerment to act in relation to their particular area of activity. The end result is pride and one of continuous improvement. The circle then continues with all elements being maintained and further developed in their own right.

Employee satisfaction

One instrument for the measurement of employee satisfaction is the attitude survey. The Royal Mail conducted its first attitude survey in 1987, but at that time senior management did not take action on the results, nor was feedback provided to the employees. However, the fact the survey was done then was extremely valuable in that it gave us an additional year of data. Surveys are now conducted annually. In fact, the performance levels have shown from that 1987 level, a decline in 1988, a further decline in 1989 when the total quality approach was just being introduced at the top of the business but was not broadly understood, an improvement in 1990, which in virtually all areas took the performance level above that of 1987 and in most areas a further improvement in 1991. It is worth noting that in 1992 some employee attitude parameters showed a slight downturn, particularly for managers. The data is shown for the period 1989–92 in Figure 7.9. While the uncertainty created by the major changes implemented in 1992 (and described later) can be used to 'explain', that is not an acceptable reason and hence more focus must be provided in this area.

Key Measurements 1989–92

satisfaction with communications
(% very/fairly satisfied)

	1989	1990	1991	1992
Managers	42%	49%	57%	55%
Non-managers	36%	43%	49%	51%

Royal Mail recognizes good work
(% agreeing strongly/slightly)

Managers	22%	35%	57%	52%
Non-managers	12%	25%	37%	35%

Royal Mail believes employees important
(% agreeing strongly/slightly)

Managers	26%	46%	52%	47%
Non-managers	14%	32%	36%	37%

Figure 7.9   Employee attitude survey, 1989–92

Management actions and behaviours

A critical element in any total quality direction is the whole area of the behaviour and action of management. The Royal Mail traditionally has been a hierarchical organization with certain militaristic approaches. For example, the use of the terms 'leave', 'officer' and 'duty' have been commonplace. One of the key changes required, if the organization is to become customer-focused, is for managers at all levels of the organization to recognize that a key activity is for them to provide support to those who 'work for them' in terms of the organization. This is a reverse of the traditional view often held that individuals work for their boss. In fact the primary role of the manager, in relation to those who work for him or her, is for the manager to satisfy their support requirements, so that those working for him or her are able to achieve their own objectives and so meet the requirements of their customers.

We are all 'superb managers' until we receive effective feedback on our performance. This feedback has been achieved through the Management Behaviour Feedback System. This system was first used after a manager has led his or her team in the Customer First workshop (i.e. the total quality workshop). It is then used on a regular basis, no more than six-monthly but at least once a year, thereafter. The feedback system allows a manager to perform a self-assessment in respect of 25 basic behaviours that are measured in terms of how effectively he or she meets the requirements of his or her colleagues who work for the manager in organizational terms. Those who work for the manager also provide feedback in similar terms, entering their responses through a micro-computer system. The system produces a printout, which is discussed by the manager and the relevant Quality Support Manager. The data is then presented back to the team members at a team meeting and a discussion ensues as to how improvement can be achieved. In the vast majority of cases improvement requires not only change of action by the manager but also by team members, and the way that they work together.

The rating categories that are established in terms of meeting requirements are shown below:

A   Frequency very low.
B   Frequency below requirement; effectiveness below requirement.
C1 Frequency below requirement; effectiveness meets requirement.
C2 Frequency meets requirement; effectiveness below requirement.
D   Frequency meets requirement; effectiveness meets requirement.

The C categories show that it is quite possible for a manager to not display a particular behaviour sufficiently frequently but be very good at it when he or she does so; the reverse is also true – that the frequency requirements can be met but there are deficiencies in terms of effectiveness.

Organizational roles and responsibilities

While total quality can only be achieved through the line organization, in order to achieve the change there is a need for a support framework to exist within the organization. That framework consists of Quality Support Managers who were positioned as full time members of the 85 key teams that drove the Royal Mail in its pre-April 1992 organizational structure. The same principle has been maintained in the new structure. The majority of those 85 Quality Support Managers were recruited from within the business and introduced progressively as the cascade of total quality took place in the organization, starting in January of 1989. Those Quality Support Managers on recruitment went through a seven-week training programme, five weeks of which were spent off the job at the Post Office College at Milton Keynes. While these Quality Support Managers report directly to the key senior managers of the organization, they have also worked together in a very strong network to ensure the maintenance of the principles of total quality as agreed for Royal Mail throughout the organization. However, this approach also allowed for local priorities to be established and actioned.

Training

The training activity associated with total quality has been the largest management training activity undertaken by the Royal Mail. For all senior and middle managers, five-day workshops (split up into three phases of 1 day, 2 days and 2 days) took place in a cascade format, starting with the team of the Managing Director, Bill Cockburn. Every other senior and middle manager has had a double involvement, first as a team member and then leading his/her own team through the workshop. For the first-line managers, particularly in operational areas, a modular approach, with modules normally lasting half a day, has been adopted to meet the operations requirements of the business. The cascade to all managers was completed by March 1992.

During October 1991 the approach to operational employees was piloted with 2000 employees. Communication and awareness training has been completed for all operational employees during financial year 1992–3. Specific skills training is provided when operational employees participate in improvement activities. Some 6000 improvement projects have been active in 1992–3.

The five-day training is broken down into three phases. The first phase concentrates on some basic concepts of quality, and allows these to be discussed. Most importantly, the first day focuses on the identification of: why the particular group exists, what actual hard tangible outputs it produces and who are the customers for these outputs from the team. For many teams, particularly the management teams of the business, this was the first time that there had been clear definition of why they exist and what value they add within the organization. Between phases one and two, team members are asked to take these outputs and to discuss them with people who they have perceived as customers and then report back at the start of phase two. The basic principle of these early steps in total quality for Royal Mail has been 'You improve what it is you do.' In consequence, it has been of significant importance that we get clear definitions of what people working in team or work groups actually produce. Phase two focuses on how improvement can be achieved using the improvement process and the related tools and techniques of improvement. Much of this phase can then be devoted to considering improvement of the outputs that the team has identified as its own.

Phase three emphasizes the skills and processes associated with team work and places particular emphasis on management actions and behaviour. A key component of management action and behaviours has been specific training in respect of recognition skills. So important has this been that in some areas of the organization this particular module has been cascaded ahead of the broad cascade of the training workshops.

Customer-focused performance improvement

A key factor in this area which makes the Royal Mail approach different is the emphasis on improvement rather than problem solving. By tradition, we have been a failure- rather than recognition-focused organization. If one addresses change from the context of problem solving, there is a tradition of identifying those responsible for failure. However, all the analytical tools associated with problem solving are incorporated into the improvement process.

We have also emphasized the identification of improvement opportunities, which come from six key areas. Those areas include customer and employee feedback, but also techniques such as cost of quality and benchmarking. Cost

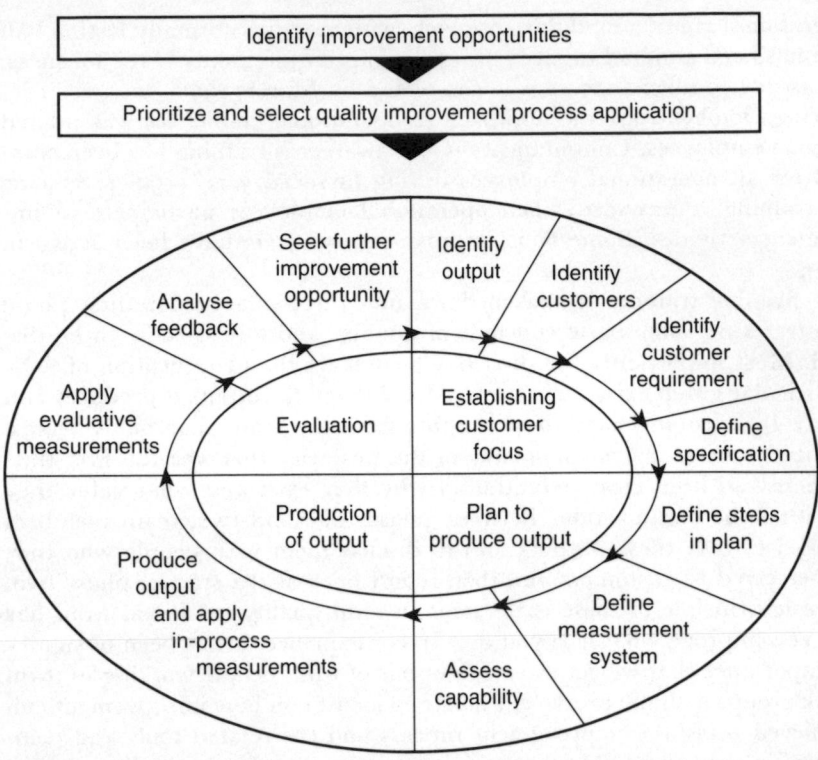

Figure 7.10 Customer-focused performance improvement.

of quality is only used as an identifier of improvement opportunities and not as a financial factor.

Figure 7.10 represents the basic process, showing the need to identify improvement opportunities and to prioritize and select those areas for improvement. The improvement process provides for a common language throughout the organization. It is a simple process of identifying the area (output) to be improved, focusing that area towards the customers, planning to produce the output, producing the output and then evaluating its effectiveness.

Management process

It is the management process that holds together all the elements of the total quality direction. This is particularly true, as included within the overall banner of management process are the business planning and performance review processes. The management process of Royal Mail is undergoing continuous development with major change occurring in line with the organizational change titled 'Business Development' (and described later).

Benchmarking

In October 1990 it was felt that many of the senior management in the business would benefit by being exposed to the progress made by organizations further down the total quality track. In consequence, senior managers visited organizations in the USA that had either achieved or were considered major candidates for the US quality award, the Baldrige Award. The team followed a structured process in relation to a benchmarking process, which has been developed for use within the business. As a consequence, they became the first 'model' users of the benchmarking process. Their activities before, during and after the visits were documented and communicated to provide a model of the use of the process.

Amongst the key factors to emerge were an understanding of what can be achieved and, most importantly, the belief that the basic steps that have been, and are being taken in the Royal Mail, are providing an appropriate foundation for achieving those longer-term objectives. The benchmarking visits in October 1990 and February 1991 were crucial to the next step in the Royal Mail pursuit of total quality, what we called 'business development'.

In December 1990, Bill Cockburn presented to the Board of the Post Office and then to the Senior Managers of Royal Mail, the broad context of the way forward for the Business. This was described under the generic title of Business Development and was presented in terms of a vision. The target date for achieving this vision was set at April 1992. Figure 7.11 shows the intended benefits of the change and takes us back to our mission and our Total Quality direction.

Business Development emphasizes the five strategies derived from the mission, namely the customer, the employee, our operational processes and profitability plus the strategy that describes our overall way of working, namely total quality. It is our intent to be closer to the customer by managing through postcode areas while at the same time simplifying our organization in terms of its structure. Our internal organization is of no interest to the external customer. By moving to a small strategic headquarters and the formation of nine geographical divisions and four strategic business units, each with devolved accountabilities, it will be possible for us to place greater emphasis on the definition and improvement of our business processes. In that sense people working as individuals or in teams will understand how their outputs are part of an overall process that focuses towards the external customer. Consequently their improvement activities will be integrated into the improvement of the overall process. While we have already placed emphasis on measurement, that emphasis will further increase through the years ahead. Business Development reinforces the direction that Royal Mail is taking in terms of its total quality approach, based on putting the customer first.

The principal aims of Business Development are to

- Move closer to the customer in terms of products and effective interfaces.
- Simplify the organization and reduce bureaucracy.

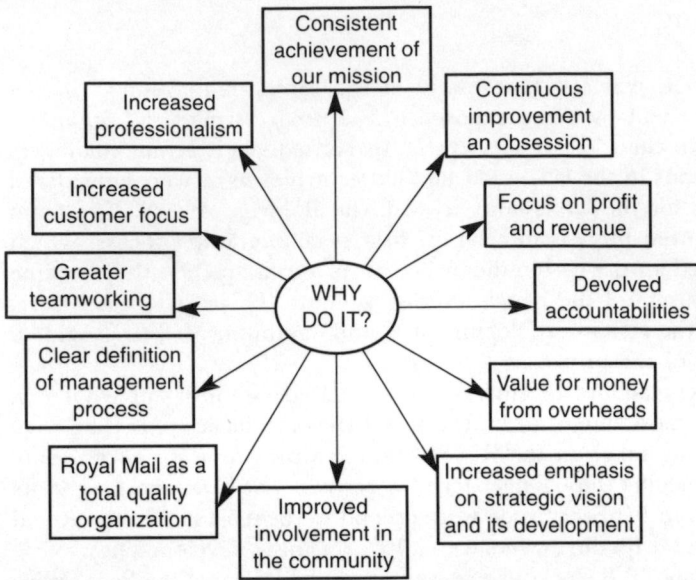

Figure 7.11   Business development. The need to change – intended benefits.

- Focus on the five strategies derived from the Mission, namely the customer, the employee, our operational processes, profitability plus the strategy that describes the overall way of working, namely total quality.

The change was managed by the Royal Mail executive team as the steering group supported by a full-time lead role director and team. This direction and team were supported by an interlinked network of focus groups involving over 1000 managers.

In April 1991 no managers knew what job they would be occupying in April 1992. Some 10,000 managers, including Bill Cockburn and his team, went through assessment systems. There was also a very open communication system and a determination to achieve all 1991–2 business targets whilst managing the change. In fact all targets were achieved.

This massive change undoubtedly created tensions and uncertainty within the business. While this was recognized and efforts made to minimize the impact, we were not completely successful as demonstrated by the attitude survey scores for 1992. However, these actions were considered key to our further development as a customer-focused business.

The key outcomes of business development, introduced on schedule in April 1992 are the following:

- Manage the business through 120 postcode areas rather than 64 districts.
- Group those 120 postcode areas into 9 geographical divisions, with divisions accountable for customer satisfaction, employee satisfaction, product 'end-to-end' performance and contribution/profit.

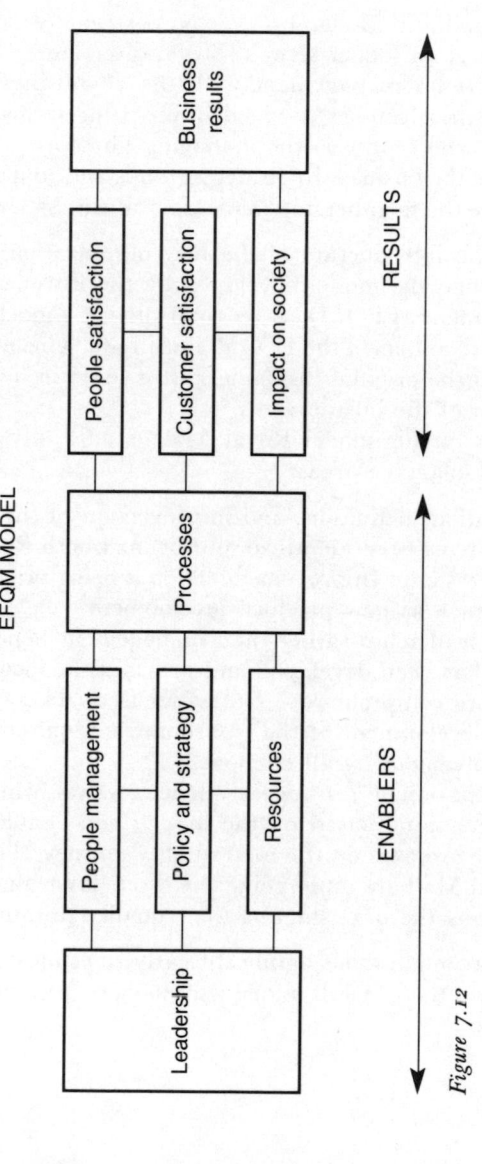

Figure 7.12

- Create four strategic business units that focus on particular sectors of the market and five business centres that provide key support services such as catering, engineering and construction, and research and development.
- Move to wider spans of control with three layers of management removed in many areas.
- Headquarters reduced in size by over 90 per cent (2100 –> 160) with increased emphasis on longer-term strategic direction.
- Change to portfolio management with the 18 business units (divisions, SBUs, and business centres) divided in reporting terms between the strategic directors who report to the managing director.
- Management of the business by strategy groups and supporting focus groups with the bulk of the membership made up of Business Unit representatives.

At the time of the introduction of the new organization in April 1992 the Royal Mail adopted the model developed by the European Foundation for Quality Management (EFQM) as its total quality model. The Royal Mail have been active members of the EFQM since 1989. This model (Figure 7.12) is consistent with the original 'fishbone' but is more in line with the current state of evolution of the business.

In the context of this model Royal Mail is currently placing particular emphasis on the following areas:

1. The identification, definition, and improvement of the key business processes. These have been identified and defined both Royal Mail-wide and for each business unit. Improvement action is being prioritized in a number of key areas such as new product development.
2. Emphasizing leadership rather than management behaviours. A Leadership Charter has been developed and provides the focus for further training and a more comprehensive behaviour feedback system.
3. The further development of the environment required to encourage and maintain involvement by all employees.
4. The implementation of business excellence reviews, which represent a self-assessment technique based on the model, and enable business units to establish their progress on the total quality journey. The 200 senior managers of Royal Mail are undergoing the three-day training as assessors for these reviews as the next stage of their quality training.

Royal Mail has made some significant early steps on its total quality journey but recognizes there is still a long way to go to become a truly customer-focused business.

8

Quality in Higher Education: An International Perspective

Malcolm Frazer

Introduction

During the last decade, many countries have experienced a growing concern for quality in higher education. The manifestations of this concern and the reasons for it vary from country to country. Much depends on the culture and history of the country and its state of economic development. Clearly, it would not be possible in this short chapter to provide a systematic review and evaluation of the principles and processes of quality assurance for each country. Instead some common themes will be illustrated by reference to a selection of countries:

1. Australia.[1]
2. France.[2]
3. Germany.[3]
4. Hong Kong.[4]
5. India.[5]
6. The Netherlands.[6]
7. New Zealand.[7]
8. Republic of South Africa.[8]
9. United Kingdom.[9]
10. United States of America.[10]

Reasons for the concern for quality in higher education

The concern for quality in higher education comes from several quarters:

1. Government, which in most countries is the paymaster.
2. Citizens, who pay taxes to government.
3. Employers of graduates.

4. Students and their parents.
5. Teachers, professors and managers in universities.[11]

Government and taxpayers (including employers) are concerned about rising costs and the priority to give to higher education within the long list of other socially desirable activities, for example: nursery, primary, secondary and vocational education, health care and social security. The 'snowball' effect, arising from parents in one generation having experienced higher education and wanting it for their children, has led to an increasing demand, which many countries have tried to meet by increasing the number of places available. 'More does not mean worse', but those who pay, and those who study, want evidence to support this assertion, and those who teach and manage in universities have a responsibility to provide the evidence. This first reason for the concern is a financial one, that is 'value for money'.

The second reason is about effectiveness. In many countries the expansion of higher education has not brought the prosperity some promised it would. There are well-known examples of developing countries that undertook massive expansion of higher education only to discover that there were many unemployed, underemployed, or misemployed graduates who were disillusioned and often a focus for discontent. In other countries, employers complain about the inability of graduates to contribute to their enterprises. Horror stories circulate of innumerate and illiterate graduates with high expectations but minds filled with knowledge that cannot be used. Whether such stories are true or not, their circulation has led to a demand from those outside higher education for the quality of courses to be exposed, and from those within for an urgency to check, change if necessary and demonstrate the value of their courses.

This leads to the third reason for the concern for quality. Higher education has been seen by many as 'a secret garden'. Better communications, nationally and internationally, and more openness in many other fields of activity have meant that universities can no longer hide behind the defence of academic freedom. Universities need to expose and to explain to society at large what they are about and how well they are doing it.

The fourth and final reason is due to the lowering of national barriers by political change, by massive increase in travel and by the electronic communications revolution. Each of these has had an effect on higher education. Government wants students to learn in, from and about other countries. Students themselves want to be more mobile. This has produced a need to understand the equivalences of qualifications, the standards reached and the values to be attached to credit for something learnt in one country to be transferred to another.

In summary, quality in higher education is important because universities must be accountable to society, to employers, to students, and to each other (Figure 8.1). The accountability is not merely financial. Universities exist to generate new knowledge, to disseminate knowledge and to safeguard and transmit a cultural heritage. However, before any international comparisons

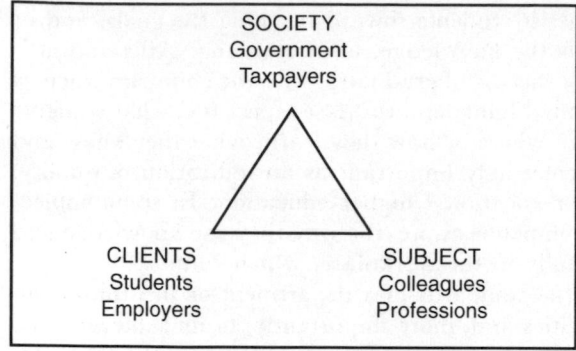

Figure 8.1 Accountability in higher education.

of the different approaches to accountability can be made it is important to be clear about what is meant, and not meant, by quality in higher education.

Some meanings of quality

It is strange that, although there is clearly an international consensus that quality in higher education is important, there is no agreement either between, or within, countries about what is meant by quality. De Weert,[12] by reference to France, the Netherlands, the UK and the US, analyses some meanings to be attached to quality.

It is clear that quality in higher education is a pervasive but elusive concept. It is multi-faceted and embraces three broad aspects: (i) goals; (ii) the process deployed for achieving goals; and (iii) how far goals are achieved. There is no single definition or way of measuring quality. The best that can be done is for experienced people to make judgements about each of these three aspects and the interactions between them. The goals, processes and achievements can refer to institutions, to parts of institutions (faculties, departments, course teams) or to individual researchers and teachers. But above all quality must be about scholarship and learning.

Much confusion would be avoided if there could be agreement internationally on the meaning of terms related to, but not the same as, quality. Some of these terms are level, standards, effectiveness and efficiency:

1. Level. A doctorate programme is at a higher level than one leading to a baccalaureate. This does not mean that doctoral programmes are of higher quality than baccalaureate programmes.
2. Standards. These are statements defining the threshold that must be reached before programmes can be offered or qualifications can be awarded. For a specified level, standards may be statements about: (i) goals, that is the knowledge, understanding, skills and attitudes it is intended that students should attain; and/or (ii) facilities, that is the staff, buildings, libraries,

equipment available to assist students toward reaching the goals; and/or (iii) achievements, that is the knowledge, understanding, skills and attitudes actually attained by successful graduates. In some countries, such as New Zealand and the United Kingdom, this last aspect (i.e. what students know and can do, and not where or how they learnt what they know and can do), is becoming increasingly important as an indication of quality. This is especially true for vocational higher education. In some subject areas it is the students' competences, i.e. the way they use knowledge and skills to perform successfully in the workplace, which counts.

At the research level, the standards of a department or institution can also be related to its facilities and, more importantly, to its achievements. In most countries, the latter is measured to some extent by the quantity, depth, stimulation and actual or potential utility of the new knowledge and ideas generated.

3. Effectiveness. This is a measure of the match between stated goals and their achievement. It is always possible to achieve 'easy', low-standard goals. In other words, quality in higher education cannot only be a question of achievements 'outputs' but must also involve judgements about the goals (part of 'inputs').

4. Efficiency. This is a measure of the resources used (costs) to achieve stated goals. It is unfortunate that governments frequently confuse quality in higher education with efficiency. Low-standard goals might well be achieved at low cost.

To illustrate the complex nature of the concept of quality in higher education, let us imagine a number of departments in different universities producing graduates in the same subject at the same level. Let us further imagine that, on average, the standard of achievement (competences) of the graduates from each department are equivalent. Are the departments of equivalent quality? The perception of the public (government officials, employers, parents and students) would probably be that the departments differ in quality. But because there are different criteria for quality it would be foolish to attempt to place the departments in order of quality. Department A attracts students on entry with the highest possible grades, whereas Department B attracts students on entry with much lower grades. The public perception is that A is of higher quality than B. But because the achievements of the graduates are the same, it could be argued that B is of higher quality because the 'value added' to its students is much greater. Department C has better qualified staff and better physical facilities than Department D. The public perception is that C is of higher quality than D. But C is more costly and, because the achievements of the graduates are the same, D is more efficient. Department E proclaims goals of high standards whereas Department F is more modest in its statements of what it intends. The public perception of E is that it is of higher quality than F, whereas F is more effective than E.

In summary, quality in higher education is a complex idea, but above all it is about what students have learnt (what they know, what they can do and what their attitudes are) as a result of their interactions with their teachers, department and university. A short list of the desired general characteristics of what should be learnt in higher education includes:

1. Love and respect for scholarship.
2. Love and respect for the subject and a desire to see the subject used to help society.
3. Desire to know more about the subject.
4. Competence in the subject consistent with the course aims.
5. Knowing how to learn.
6. Knowing the limits of their knowledge and skills.
7. Realization that learning is a life-long process.
8. Problem solving or opportunity taking (i.e. problem recognition, definition and formulation of solutions, or approaches to solutions).
9. Knowing how to find out (i.e. how to use libraries and other databases).
10. Formulating an argument.
11. Integrating knowledge from different fields.
12. Communication skills (writing and reading; speaking and listening).
13. Critical analysis.
14. Working in a team.

Quality assurance – terminology

As there is no international agreement concerning the meaning of quality in higher education, it is not surprising that there is confusion about the terms used to describe various activities aimed at maintaining and enhancing quality. At an international conference on quality assurance in higher education the author attempted to define the most frequently used terms.[13] This attempt is summarized in the following paragraphs.

Quality control

Clearly every enterprise needs to have a system to check whether the raw materials it uses, the products it makes, or the services it provides, reach minimum predefined (threshold) standards, so that the substandard can be rejected. Long ago, industry learnt that this form of quality control was not enough. Most employees felt that the quality of the product or service was not their responsibility, that it did not matter if a substandard product was passed to the controllers, and that improving quality was not their concern. Industry, therefore, introduced the concept of quality assurance.

Quality assurance

As defined in this chapter, and by many in industry, quality assurance has four components. These are that:

1. Everyone in the enterprise has a responsibility for maintaining the quality of the product or service (i.e. the substandard rarely reaches the quality controllers because they have been rejected at source).
2. Everyone in the enterprise has a responsibility for enhancing the quality of the product or service.
3. Everyone in the enterprise understands, uses and feels ownership of the systems that are in place for maintaining and enhancing quality.
4. Management (and sometimes the customer or client) regularly checks the validity and reliability of the systems for checking quality.

If the word university replaces enterprise throughout this paragraph, then a university that takes quality assurance seriously emerges as a self-critical community of students, teachers, support staff and senior managers, each contributing to and striving for continued improvement.

Quality audit

A scrutiny by a group external to the university checking that the quality assurance and quality control processes are appropriate and working properly has been described as 'quality audit'. The concept of quality audit has been developed in the United Kingdom. In 1990 the Committee of Vice-Chancellors and Principals established a small Academic Audit Unit using experienced academics on temporary secondment from universities.[14] Recent proposals from the UK Government[15] include the establishment of a Quality Audit Unit with a somewhat similar role. Quality audit is neither concerned with a university's mission (objectives, inputs) nor with how successfully these objectives have been attained (outputs), but solely with the processes by which the university checks on the relations between its inputs and outputs.

Accreditation

This term is most frequently used in the United States. Accreditation can apply either to institutions or to programmes (subject or professional areas). Chernay[16] describes the purposes of accreditation as follows:

Accreditation assures the educational community, the general public, and other agencies or organisations that an institution or programme (a) has clearly defined and educationally appropriate objectives, (b) maintains conditions under which their achievement can reasonably be expected, (c) is in fact accomplishing them substantially, and (d) can be expected to continue to do so.

It is noteworthy that in this definition of accreditation there is no requirement to judge whether the objectives of an institution or programme are to meet any specified, or threshold standard. Description of the accreditation system in the United States seen through British eyes has been published.[17] In some countries, accreditation would imply that at least a threshold standard was intended and being achieved. For example, in the United Kingdom professional bodies accredit courses of study (programmes), meaning that graduates will be granted professional recognition.

In 1986 India set itself the task of accrediting all higher technical education by establishing a National Board of Accreditation. This is a formidable task and, if successful, the approach in India may well prove a model for other developing countries.[18]

The Council for National Academic Awards (CNAA) in the United Kingdom[19] and the Hong Kong Council for Academic Accreditation[20] use accreditation to mean that, subject to certain safeguards and to regular review, an institution is self-validating.

Validation

The process of approving a new programme, or allowing an existing programme to continue, is described as validation.[21] It is a check that predefined, minimum standards will be (new programme), or are (existing programme) reached. Most universities take responsibility for approving their own programmes and do not involve external agencies or even external individual peer reviewers. Exceptions are the 'non-university' institutions in some countries (e.g. Hong Kong, Republic of South Africa, United Kingdom).

Peer review

The involvement of people as active university teachers, as researchers or as practising professionals to offer advice and to make judgements and/or decisions about proposals for new programmes, the continuation or modification of existing programmes, the quality of research programmes or the quality of institutions is described as peer review. All the countries mentioned in this paper use peer review to some extent in their processes for quality maintenance and enhancement in higher education.

Quality assessment and quality measurement

For most products or services it is clearly possible to define, nationally or internationally, a minimum acceptable or threshold standard. For example, it is possible to specify the percentage vitamin C in orange juice, the fuel consumption of a car or the number of trains arriving within x minutes of the scheduled time. If there is a single parameter defining the standard then quality control is simple. Furthermore, if there are a number of similar products or services, applying the measurement enables them to be compared and even put in rank order. For example, orange juice from a number of manufacturers could be put in rank order based on the percentage of vitamin C, with some perhaps falling below the threshold. However, there would be little point in comparing, and then placing in rank order samples of orange juice and mineral water because mineral water is not purchased for its vitamin C. Furthermore, vitamin C content is not the only quality parameter for orange juice. Others might be the percentage of sugar, of other sweeteners, of 'orange flavouring', to say nothing of more subjective factors such as taste. Quality in higher education is like quality in orange juice, it is multifaceted. Thus, it is better to consider a 'quality profile' than to give a single measure for quality. The profile could be in the form of a bar chart of measurements on several predetermined characteristics. The profile might describe an individual teacher, a programme, a department or even the whole university.

The UK has introduced legislation to establish quality assessment committees to advise the higher education funding councils.[22] However, quality assessment or measurement should not be associated only with decisions about funding. It can be used for other purposes. For example, the Australian Vice-Chancellors' Committee has established Academic Standards Panels, which are reviewing the curriculum, assessment and grading statistics in each university in a number of subject areas (for example physics, history, psychology and computer science).

There are confusions about quality measurement in higher education. It is sometimes assumed that quality measurement involves people *external* to the university assigning *objective, quantitative* scores or performance indicators, which are then *norm-referenced* (i.e. the measures are relative to other universities, leading to comparisons by placing them in a rank order or in bands; for example excellent, good, normal, poor and bad). Each of the words in italics will be taken in turn.

Quality measurement does not have to be made by *externals*. It is very desirable, as part of a university's quality assurance activities, that members of the university make measurements of particular characteristics of quality, for example the number of students obtaining course-related employment within six months of graduating. If a national performance indicator is available for this characteristic, then the university can see where it stands in comparison to other universities.

Quality measurement does not have to involve an *objective, quantitative* score. To return to the example of orange juice and the characteristic of taste. An orange juice manufacturer will assemble a panel of experts and consumers, train them and then, under carefully controlled and 'fair' conditions, ask them to make judgements about the taste of different samples. The responses of the panel might be converted to scores, but nevertheless they remain judgements. In respect of universities the panel might consist of academic peers, students and employers.

Quality measurement does not have to be *norm-referenced*. For any characteristic of quality it would be possible to define criteria (standards) to be met. The university (or department, programme, individual teacher) then either meets the criteria (passes) or does not meet the criteria (fails) for the particular characteristic.

Quality assurance – purposes

Before undertaking any evaluation of quality in higher education it is essential to be clear about the purpose. There can also be confusion about the roles of the various agencies concerned with quality unless their purpose is properly understood. Each agency can be positioned within the triangle in Figure 8.1 according to its main purpose. For example, a funding body would be near the apex, whereas validating and accrediting bodies would be closer to the base. Purposes of evaluating quality include: (i) contributing to decisions on planning or funding; (ii) validating; (iii) granting professional recognition to programmes; (iv) accrediting; and (v) making awards of degrees. Whichever of these it is, the overriding purpose is always to maintain and enhance quality.

These different purposes can be illustrated by reference to some examples of agencies in different countries (Figure 8.2). They are classified according to whether they are owned by the universities themselves, by government or are independent.

Quality assurance – essential features

Whatever the differences in terminology and purpose it is common ground for each country that real and enduring quality can only come by actions of the universities themselves. The basis for these actions must be self-evaluation. Inspection and quality control imposed solely from outside would not work. Self-evaluation – seeing oneself – is never easy but without three aids it is virtually impossible. The first aid is a 'mirror', that is external assistance. The work of quality assurance agencies (accrediting and validating bodies, audit units and inspectors) is largely to help those engaged in higher education (whether it be an individual teacher, the programme team, the department or the university) to be self-critical and reflective. The second aid is training (staff development) for the task of self-evaluation. Third, there is a need for national and international information, such as qualitative and quantitative performance indicators[23] as well as descriptions of best practice and innovation in teaching, learning and assessment both general and subject-specific.

These three aids have a cost, but expenditure on them should not be seen as an optional luxury but as essential with a high priority. Two reviews, written from the perspectives of different countries – France[24] and The Netherlands[25] – emphasize the importance of universities taking responsibility for their own quality. But external agencies can provide help for self-evaluation through the important ingredients of: (i) peer review;[26] (ii) training of staff, students and external peers; and (iii) intelligence on best practice elsewhere. In providing this help there is scope for much more international collaboration between these agencies as proposed and agreed at the conference in Hong Kong.[27]

University-owned agencies

- Australia – Vice-Chancellors' Committee Academic Standards Panels;[1]
- United Kingdom – Committee of Vice-Chancellors and Principals Academic Audit Unit and Division of Quality Audit.[14]

Governmental agencies (i.e. statutory bodies)

Inspecting/Evaluating

- France – Comité National d'Evaluation;[2]
- The Netherlands – Higher Vocational Education Inspectorate;[6]

Funding

- Germany – Deutsche Forschungsgemeinschaft;[3]
- UK – quality assessment committees;[22]

Validating/Accrediting

- Hong Kong – Council for Academic Accreditation;[4]
- Republic of South Africa – Certification Council for Technikon Education;[8]
- India – National Board of Accreditation;[5]

Awarding

- New Zealand – New Zealand Qualifications Authority;[7]
- UK – former Council for National Academic Awards.[19]

Non-governmental agencies

Accrediting Institutions

- United States – Middle States Association of Colleges and Schools;[16]

Accrediting Programmes (subject or professional areas)

- United States – Accreditation Board for Engineering and Technology.[16]

Figure 8.2   Examples of agencies concerned with quality.

Notes and references

1. Australian Vice-Chancellors' Committee (1990) *Report on Physics by the Academic Standards Panel.* Australian Vice-Chancellors' Committee; Kwong, L.D. (1992) Academic standards panels in Australia. In Craft, A. (ed.) *Quality Assurance in Higher Education.* London, Falmer.
2. Neave, M. (1991) *Models of Quality Assurance in Europe.* London, Council for National Academic Awards; Staropoli, A. (1987) The Comité National d'Evaluation: preliminary results of a French experiment. *European Journal of Education,* 22(2), 123–31.
3. Frackmann, E. (1992) Quality assurance in German higher education. In Craft, A. (ed.) *Quality Assurance in Higher Education.* London, Falmer.
4. Sensicle, A. (1992) The Hong Kong initiative. In Craft, A. (ed.) *Quality Assurance in Higher Education.* London, Falmer.

5. Chandra. A. (1992) Towards accreditation in Indian higher technical education. In Craft, A. (ed.) *Quality Assurance in Higher Education*. London, Falmer.

6. Neave, M. (1991), see note 2; Kalkijyk, J. and Vroeijenstijn, T.I. (1992) Perspective from the Netherlands. In Craft, A. (ed.) *Quality Assurance in Higher Education*. London, Falmer; Vroeijenstijn, T.I. (1990) Autonomy and assurance of quality: two sides of one coin. *Higher Education Research and Development*, 9, 1.

7. New Zealand Qualifications Authority (NZQA) (1991) *Developing the National Qualifications Framework*. Wellington, NZQA.

8. Certification Council for Technikon Education (SERTEC) (1991) *Manual for the Evaluation of Standards at Technikons*. Pretoria, Republic of South Africa, SERTEC.

9. Department of Education and Science (1991) *Higher Education: A National Framework*. London, HMSO; Harris, R.W. (1990) The CNAA accreditation and quality assurance. *Higher Education Review*, 23(3), 34–53; Williams, P. (1992) The UK academic audit unit. In Craft, A. (ed.) *Quality Assurance in Higher Education*. London, Falmer.

10. Adelman, C. and Silver, H. (1990) *Accreditation: The American Experience*. London, Council for National Academic Awards; Benmark, L. (1992) The accreditation of engineering education in the US. In Craft, A. (ed.) *Quality Assurance in Higher Education*. London, Falmer; Chernay, G. (1990) *Accreditation and the Role of the Council on Postsecondary Accreditation (COPA)*. Washington DC, COPA; Department of Education and Science (1991) *Aspects of Education in the USA. Quality and its Assurance in Higher Education*. London, HMSO; Middle States Association of Colleges and Schools (1990) *Characteristics of Excellence in Higher Education – Standards for Accreditation*. Pennsylvania, Commission on Higher Education of the Middle States Association; Peace Lenn, M. (1992) The role of accreditation in American higher education. In Craft, A. (ed.) *Quality Assurance in Higher Education*. London, Falmer.

11. For convenience, 'university' is used throughout this article to include all types of institution (colleges, polytechnics, technical and vocational institutes, universities, etc.) providing higher education.

12. De Weert, E. (1990) A macro-analysis of quality assessment in higher education. *Higher Education*, 19, 57–72.

13. Frazer, M.J. (1992) Quality assurance in higher education. In Craft, A. (ed.) *Quality Assurance in Higher Education*. London, Falmer.

14. Williams, P. (1992), see note 9.

15. DES (1991), see note 9.

16. Chernay, G. (1990), see note 10.

17. Adelman, C. and Silver, H. (1990), see note 10.

18. Chandra, A. (1992), see note 5.

19. Harris, R.W. (1990), see note 9.

20. Sensicle, A. (1992), see note 4.

21. Church, C.H. (1988) The qualities of validation. *Studies in Higher Education*, 13(1), 27–44.

22. DES (1991), see note 9.

23. Johnes, J. and Taylor, J. (1990) *Performance Indicators in Higher Education*. Buckingham, The Society for Research into Higher Education and Open University Press.

24. Staropoli, A. (1987), see note 2.

25. Vroeijenstijn, T.I. (1990), see note 6.

26. Acherman, H.A. (1990) Quality assessment by peer review a new area for university cooperation. *Higher Education Management*, 2(2), 179–92.

27. Frazer, M.J. (1992), see note 13.

9

Looking Ahead

Diana Green

One of the risks facing an editor who commissions contributions on a topical issue is that the policy agenda will change during the process of compilation. This book is no exception to that rule. The purpose of this brief postscript is therefore to summarize developments in the quality assessment area since the 1992 Act.

The policy context

Each of the three regional Higher Education Funding Councils (HEFC) has established a Quality Assessment Committee to advise it on its statutory obligation under the 1992 Act to assess the quality of higher education. The English and Scottish Councils consulted institutions about the assessment method they planned to use in the Autumn of 1992. That proposed by the English Funding Council (HEFC(E)), based on a series of pilot assessments carried out jointly by the PCFC and the UFC earlier in the year, proved to be more controversial than the Scottish model. Also, in the Autumn of 1992, the HEFC(E) decided to carry out six further test assessments, three each in the areas of business and management, and law. The purpose was to develop further and evaluate the assessment rather than carry out 'live' assessments. Following an analysis of the results of these and of the responses to the consultation exercise, a circular was issued in January 1993 describing progress with the assessment method and setting out a timetable for the assessment of quality in the first four subject areas: chemistry, history, law and mechanical engineering. These first assessments are scheduled to be completed by December 1993, in order to inform funding in 1994–5. It is planned that a further four assessments (in architecture, business and management, computer science and social work) will be undertaken before September 1994 in order to inform funding decisions in 1995–6.

Given the critical response of the English universities to the consultation exercise, the HEFC(E) has sought to reassure institutions that assessment should be seen as positive and facilitative. While the Council is obliged to ensure that all the education it funds is of at least satisfactory quality and to ensure that unsatisfactory provision is rectified speedily, it also seeks to reward excellence and encourage quality improvements by the publication of assessment reports. In describing the principles that underlie the assessment method, the HEFC(E) recognizes:

1. That teaching and learning are inseparable.
2. That quality of teaching and learning in a diverse sector can only be understood in the context of an institution's own aims and objectives.
3. That quality should be assessed both in terms of student achievement and the totality of the learning experience.
4. That quality can be described by reference to a number of dimensions or criteria (for example, the quality of staff, learning support facilities, student and employer satisfaction, value added).
5. That the various stakeholders (students, teachers, institutions, employers) will weight these criteria differently.

The assessment method has two main elements: institutional self-assessment in the particular subject and an assessment visit by a team of assessors. Both elements will be informed by an initial analysis of statistical data currently collected nationally.

Unlike quality audit, which focuses on systems and procedures, quality assessment is subject-based. The Council has indicated that it does not intend to visit all institutions in all subjects. Priority will be given to those claiming their provision is excellent and those where there are grounds for concern that quality in a particular subject is at risk.

Where assessment has taken place, provision will be rated as falling into one of three categories: excellent, satisfactory or unsatisfactory.

Universities retain a significant degree of scepticism and concern about the assessment exercise, despite the changes that followed the consultation. While the emphasis on the importance and diversity of institutional mission has to some extent alleviated the concerns about inappropriate comparisons (say, Oxbridge colleges with 'new' universities in the inner cities), a residual fear remains that the results of assessment exercises will be used to construct 'league tables' purporting to rank high- and low-quality institutions. This is exacerbated by the decision to rate assessments. Whatever the validity and reliability of the judgements made, institutions have been quick to see how those 'fortunate' to have been assessed in the first round might use their ratings to secure a competitive advantage. However, the area of greatest concern remains the link between quality assessment and funding.

In its response to the HEFC(E), the Committee for Vice-Chancellors and Principals urged the Council to delay meeting its statutory obligation (which, it argued, was not time-constrained) until it had produced a more credible methodology. The Council appears to have partly conceded this, insofar as it has agreed that there is a need to be cautious about the impact of the link between funding and an excellent grade. However, it is more likely that the decision reflects a pragmatic response to a change in Government policy. Briefly, the funding methodology for the new unified sector announced by the HEFC(E) was a strategy designed to promote further growth in student numbers, in line with the Government's aim of increasing the participation rate. Similarly, quality assessment was designed to ensure that funding for growth was directed to those institutions whose provision was assessed as excellent. The announcement by the Government in its 1992 Autumn Statement that the growth of higher education is to be capped is a major setback. The reasons for the decision were obvious:

1. The strategy of promoting growth had proved too successful. If expansion continued at the current rate, the desired participation rate (one in three) would be achieved by 1996, rather than 2000, as planned. The public expenditure consequences of this growth, driven by the mandatory grant regulations, were not acceptable.
2. The political priority, in funding terms, had to be the successful launch of the further education institutions, newly incorporated following the 1992 Act.

Whether the Council's funding methodology can be successfully adapted for 'consolidation' and what the implications of this are for quality assessment remain open questions.

The QHE project: preliminary results

In Chapter 1, reference was made to a national project on quality assessment. During the first stage of the project, completed in October 1992,[1] a working hypothesis was developed: that quality is a relative concept. Its definition varies according to who is making the assessment, which aspect of the higher education process is being considered and the purpose for which the assessment is made. The focus of the empirical research was to identify the key stakeholders in higher education and explore what criteria they regarded as important for assessing quality. Initially, eight stakeholder groups were identified:

- students;
- employers;
- governmental (subdivided into ministerial departments – DFE, DE);
- funding Councils;
- teaching staff in higher education institutions;
- managerial staff in higher education (including bodies such as the CDP and the CVCP);
- accrediting and validating bodies (for example, BTEC);
- assessment bodies (for example, HMI).

The aim was to produce a set of quality criteria, ranked in order of preference, reflecting the views of all the stakeholders. While it was recognized that there might be differences of opinion, it was hoped that a set of core criteria would emerge around which there was a consensus. Existing quality assurance techniques would then be evaluated against these criteria in order to determine their appropriateness and usefulness in the higher education context.

Not surprisingly, differences emerged between the different stakeholder groups. For example, for employers a key criterion is that there should be effective links with employers as means of influencing the character of programmes of study. While the funding councils also regard this as important, it does not figure amongst those of their university staff or students. Nor is it a key criterion for quality assessment as far as Government departments are concerned. Similarly, most groups give a high priority, at the level of the programme of study, to the development of transferable knowledge and skills. However, there are differences between the groups about the relative importance of different skills and, within the employer group, no consensus about the desirable balance between skills and subject-specific knowledge.

Despite these differences of opinion, ten criteria were endorsed by at least four stakeholder groups as important in quality assessment:

1. There are adequate physical resources (library resources, workshops, IT resources) to support teaching and learning.
2. There are adequate human resources to support teaching and learning and staff are properly qualified.
3. Programmes of study should have clear aims and objectives, which are understood by staff and students.
4. The subject content relates to a programme's aims and objectives.
5. Students are encouraged to be actively involved in, and given responsibility for, learning.
6. The standard of the programme is appropriate to the award.
7. Assessment is valid, objective and fair.
8. Assessment covers the full range of course aims and objectives.
9. Students receive useful feedback from assessment and are kept informed of progress.
10. Students leave the programme of study with transferable knowledge and skills.

The analysis of the criteria underpinning quality assessment suggests that even if the above list could be regarded as a set of core criteria, there is no consensus among the stakeholder groups about how these should be prioritized. Thus, employers and governmental agencies put a premium on the outputs of higher education, notably what students learn and how efficient is the learning process. This emphasis on outputs is not unique to the British Government. It is a predominant feature of the assessment movement in the United States of America and a concern of governments in countries as diverse as Australia, The Netherlands and Denmark. For those within higher education, that is its staff and its students, the inputs to the educational process and the process itself are equally important. Research supports the view that a 'product'-based notion of quality may be inappropriate to education and other services and points to the need to take into account service delivery.

Quality control, audit and assessment

Like quality, quality assurance is multidimensional. In the 1991 White Paper, the Government differentiates the different processes by purpose and institutional responsibility. Thus, quality control describes the *internal* procedures for quality maintenance and enhancement. Audit and assessment involve *external* scrutiny, either of documents and procedures (audit) or the student experience and student achievement (assessment). While, in theory, the responsibilities are clearly differentiated, there is a potential overlap. As Carole Webb pointed out in Chapter 5, this is clearly a cause for concern to the universities, not least on cost grounds.

The QHE project draws some tentative conclusions about quality assessment and quality assurance. It comments on the desirable attributes of an overall methodology for assessing quality and tentatively evaluates existing methods against the quality criteria identified by the stakeholders.

In Britain and in the United States of America, demands for more explicit and open approaches to quality assurance have prompted some institutions to turn to industrial models of quality assurance, such as BS 5750 and total quality management (TQM). Most of these institutions are at an early stage of implementing these approaches. It is therefore too early to evaluate their success in improving quality.

Both BS 5750 and TQM have their origins in the manufacturing sector and are principally concerned with improving the quality of *products* by the careful identification of customers' needs and decreasing the degree of variation in the production process, thus reducing waste and rework. The aim is to have quality 'built in' rather than inspected, with quality being the responsibility of all employees.

There are some advantages to these systems. BS 5750 is an internationally recognized quality management system with a 'kitemark' that confers credibility, not least in the eyes of employers. TQM involves a primary focus on the customer's requirements. In the educational context, this places the student centre-stage. It can also be used to look at the quality of the whole organization, rather than the quality of the programmes of study.[2]

Evaluation of the literature suggests, however, that there might be some difficulties in adopting these models for higher education. First, both systems require acceptance of a definition of quality based on meeting customers' needs. There is no room for competing definitions of quality. Second, there are problems of identifying the customer and product, yet both systems rely on developing clear and unambiguous organizational objectives or product specifications.[3] Education, like other services:

- is intangible and ephemeral;
- is perishable;

- frequently involves the customer in the delivery of the product;
- is not perceived as a product by employees.[4]

This makes it difficult to standardize and 'control' the process, in the BS 5750 meaning of the term. Therefore, models derived from the manufacturing sector may prove to be inadequate when it comes to improving the 'service encounter' itself. This is a problem that education shares with other public and private services. In the last ten years, interest has grown in the development of alternative models of quality assurance for the service sector.[5] These approaches tend to place greater emphasis on those issues central to quality improvement in this sector, such as the character of the service encounter and recognition that service quality will be a balance between the expectations of the customer and their perception of the service received (such that a 'high' quality of service is one where the customer's perceptions meet or exceed their expectations).

There is little evidence, to date, that the theory and practice of service quality has had much impact on higher education.[6] At the policy level, there are signs that the Government is as keen to put the student at the heart of education as it is determined to put the patient at the heart of the Health Service. One measure of this is the decision to produce a Student's Charter, which, like the Patient's Charter, is expected to spell out the minimum standards a student can expect from the service providers. Whether this development is simply a passing fad or whether it presages a further milestone in the cultural revolution currently assailing higher education, only time will tell.

Notes and references

1. See Harvey, L., Burrows, A. and Green, D. (1992) *Criteria of Quality.* QHE.
2. Heap, J.P. and Soloman, H. (1992) *Profit and Pitfalls in Establishing a Qualytechnic.* Paper presented at the AETT Conference on Quality in Education, University of York, 6–8 April.
3. Rooney, M. (1991) *Quality Assurance in Education and Training*, unpublished paper, sponsored by the Department of Employment.
4. Sanders, I.W. and Graham, M.A. (1992) Total quality management in the hospitality industry. *Total Quality Management*, 3(3), 243–55.
5. Parasuraman, A. *et al.* (1985) A conceptual model of service quality and its implications for future research. *Journal of Marketing*, 49, 41–50.
6. See, for example, work on the Student Satisfaction Project at the University of Central England in Birmingham, also Green, D. (1990) Student satisfaction: assessing quality in higher education from the customer's view. In *Proceedings of the Second International Conference on Assessing Quality in Higher Education*, University of Tennessee.

Index

The Society for Research into Higher Education

The Society for Research into Higher Education exists to stimulate and co-ordinate research into all aspects of higher education. It aims to improve the quality of higher education through the encouragement of debate and publication on issues of policy, on the organization and management of higher education institutions, and on the curriculum and teaching methods.

The Society's income is derived from subscriptions, sales of its books and journals, conference fees and grants. It receives no subsidies, and is wholly independent. Its individual members include teachers, researchers, managers and students. Its corporate members are institutions of higher education, research institutes, professional, industrial and governmental bodies. Members are not only from the UK, but from elsewhere in Europe, from America, Canada and Australasia, and it regards its international work as amongst its most important activities.

Under the imprint *SRHE & Open University Press*, the Society is a specialist publisher of research, having some 45 titles in print. The Editorial Board of the Society's Imprint seeks authoritative research or study in the above fields. It offers competitive royalties, a highly recognizable format in both hardback and paperback and the world-wide reputation of the Open University Press.

The Society also publishes *Studies in Higher Education* (three times a year), which is mainly concerned with academic issues, *Higher Education Quarterly* (formerly *Universities Quarterly*), mainly concerned with policy issues, *Research into Higher Education Abstracts* (three times a year), and *SRHE News* (four times a year).

The Society holds a major annual conference in December, jointly with an institution of higher education. In 1991, the topic was 'Research and Higher Education in Europe', with the University of Leicester. In 1992, it was 'Learning to Effect' with Nottingham Trent University, and in 1993, 'Governments and the Higher Education Curriculum: Evolving Partnerships' at the University of Sussex in Brighton. Future conferences include in 1994, 'The Student Experience' at the University of York.

The Society's committees, study groups and branches are run by the members. The groups at present include:

Teacher Education Study Group
Continuing Education Group
Staff Development Group
Excellence in Teaching and Learning

Benefits to members

Individual

Individual members receive:

- *SRHE News*, the Society's publications list, conference details and other material included in mailings.
- Greatly reduced rates for *Studies in Higher Education* and *Higher Education Quarterly*.
- A 35% discount on all Open University Press & SRHE publications.
- Free copies of the Precedings – commissioned papers on the theme of the Annual Conference.
- Free copies of *Research into Higher Education Abstracts*.
- Reduced rates for conferences.
- Extensive contacts and scope for facilitating initiatives.
- Reduced reciprocal memberships.

Corporate

Corporate members receive:

- All benefits of individual members, plus
- Free copies of *Studies in Higher Education*.
- Unlimited copies of the Society's publications at reduced rates.
- Special rates for its members, e.g. to the Annual Conference.

Membership details: SRHE, 344–354 Gray's Inn Road, London, WCIX 8BP, UK, Tel: 071 837 7880
Catalogue: SRHE & Open University Press, Celtic Court, 22 Ballmoor, Buckingham MK18 IXW. Tel: (0280) 823388

QUALITY ASSURANCE FOR UNIVERSITY TEACHING

Roger Ellis (ed.)

Assuring quality for teaching in a time of rapid change is the major challenge facing UK universities. This informative and practical book combines review chapters with case studies within a number of comparative perspectives. The book is organized around three themes. First there are descriptions of approaches to quality assurance. These include case studies from universities of TQM and BS 5750, course validation and review, student evaluation and institutional research, together with reviews of relevant approaches from industry and health care. Quality assurance based on professionalism is also considered. Second, the characteristics of quality teaching are addressed including summaries of research evidence, the results of a unique participant study, standards generated by quality circles of staff and students and a description of distinguished teaching awards in the UK and USA. Third, approaches to the development of university teachers are covered including teaching training, staff development, appraisal and the enterprise initiative.

Contents

Part 1: Assuring quality – Quality assurance for university teaching: issues and approaches – A British Standard for university teaching? – Total quality management through BS 5750: a case study – Quality assurance in health care: the implications for university teaching – Quality assurance through course validation and review – Assuring quality through student evaluation – Institutional research and quality assurance – University teaching: a professional model for quality – Part 2: Identifying quality – Teaching styles of award-winning professors – The first distinguished teaching award in the United Kingdom – Expert teachers' perceptions of university teaching: the identification of teaching skills – Teaching standards from quality circles – Effective teaching – Part 3: Developing quality – Appraisal schemes and their contribution to quality in teaching – Staff development and quality assurance – Teacher training for university teachers? – Quality in teaching and the encouragement of enterprise – Glossary – Indexes.

Contributors

Jennifer Boore, George Brown, John Dallat, Roger Ellis, Lewis Elton, Catherine Finlay, Norman Gibson, Sandra Griffiths, Jerry M. Lewis, Saranne Magennis, Gordon Rae, Christine Saunders, Eric Saunders, Susan Storey, Maurice Stringer, Ann Tate, Elaine Thomas, Dorothy Whittington, Roger Woodward.

336pp   0 335 19025 1 (Paperback)   0 335 19026 X (Hardback)

THE LEARNING UNIVERSITY
TOWARDS A NEW PARADIGM?

Chris Duke

Chris Duke addresses issues central to the evolution and future of higher education. He examines assumptions by and about universities, their changing environments, the new terminologies and their adaptation to new circumstances. He explores how far universities *are* learning, changing and adapting; and whether they are becoming different kinds of institutions or whether only the rhetoric is altering. He is particularly concerned with how far universities, as key teaching and learning organizations, are adopting the new paradigm of lifelong learning. He discusses how far the concepts and requirements for institution-wide continuing education have been identified and internalized in institutional planning; are they, for instance, reflected in programmes of staff development (in the continuing education of staff in higher education)? *Is* a new paradigm of university education and organization really emerging?

Contents
Old assumptions and new practices – Change and higher education: the new discourse – Mission, aims and objectives – What may be new? – Out of the box: continuing education university-wide – Finishing school or service station: what mix? – Access, quality and success: old and new criteria – Staff development and organizational learning – The fallacy of the ivory tower – Appendix – Bibliography – Index.

160pp   0 335 15653 3 (Paperback)   0 335 15654 1 (Hardback)

IMPROVING HIGHER EDUCATION
TOTAL QUALITY CARE

Ronald Barnett

This book provides the first systematic exploration of the topic of quality in higher education. Ronald Barnett examines the meaning of quality and its improvement at the levels of both the institution and the course – contemporary discussion having tended to focus on one or the other, without integrating the two perspectives. He argues against a simple identification of quality assessment with numerical performance indicators *or* with academic audit *or* with the messages of the market. These are the contending definitions of the modern age, but they all contain interests tangential to the main business of higher education.

Dr Barnett offers an alternative approach which begins from a sense of educators attempting to promote an open-ended development in their students. It is this view of higher education which, he argues, should be at the heart of our thinking about quality. Quality cannot be managed, but it can be cared for. Building on the conceptual base he establishes, Dr Barnett offers proposals for action in assessing institutional performance, in reviewing the quality of course programmes, and in improving the curriculum and the character of the student experience.

Contents

256pp   335 09984 X (Paperback)   0 335 09985 8 (Hardback)